DESERT
STANDARD
TIME

DESERT STANDARD TIME

By

Greg Brannan

Relatively true tales
from the wilds of Arizona
to the hallways of Hollywood

This is a fictionalized memoir. While each story is inspired by actual events, the names of most people, places and businesses have been changed, some dialogue has been imagined and some events have been compressed in time.

Printed in the United States of America.

IBSN 978-1-105-90399-1

For Mom and Dad

ACKNOWLEDGMENTS

While I've done some writing over the years, I never attempted to self-publish. However, one of the advantages of being around a while is that, if you attempt something new, you probably know someone with first-hand experience who is willing to talk with you about it.

Fortunately for me, my friends Michael Danahy and Tom Merritt, both talented writers, have self-published before and were only too happy to share their valuable knowledge. Among the hugely helpful results of that communication was an introduction to CJ Harrison. She was kind enough to take on a rookie client and edit this book. Not only did CJ ensure that its contents were fit to print, she also made a process that could have been a daunting challenge both fun and enlightening. These three have my sincere gratitude.

Doug Brannan, Lauri Smith, Robert Hoke, Tamara Rosenberg, and BigBoy Medlin are all otherwise responsible adults who, for whatever reason, have always encouraged me to write. While some might consider that encouragement ill-advised, I would be remiss not to thank them for their many years of friendship and support.

Finally, I'd like to thank my wife, Huyen, my son, Avery, and my daughter, Leila, for providing the inspiration for this project. Thanks to them, this book has made it from a wish list fantasy to a bucket list reality. I love you guys to bits.

CONTENTS

PREFACE

This effort didn't begin with any fit of creative expression, but rather with the simple desire to better distribute home-brewed beer.

In the late 1980s, a friend and I in Phoenix were well ahead of the home brewing craze and making enough beer to offer some to friends and family during the holidays. Since many of those I worked with at entertainment companies in Los Angeles and New York qualified as friends, I happily included them and unwittingly created a demand for the annual holiday brew swag.

By 1993, my friend was married and starting a family while I was heading off to work at a new job in Los Angeles alone. He suggested I take our brewing gear and keep the tradition alive. It took more gusto than I could muster to make a variety of brews alone, however, and I opted instead to put one oversized 16-ounce bottle into my holiday offering.

Another result of my solitary LA existence was a newfound passion for writing short stories about my rural past. So with beer in hand, I took a box, jammed it with genuine, edible, in-shell packing peanuts, and included a half-dozen short stories. I billed it as "Tall Tales & Stout Beer" and promised it would complement hot, greasy food. The beer always proved popular but I was pleasantly surprised by how my stories were received, so I continued writing as my schedule allowed.

Then, in the fall of 2007, I was diagnosed with an incurable form of cancer and given the usual discouraging survival statistics. With my children only seven and five years old at the time, I focused my energy on them. I've stayed as healthy as possible and addressed other priorities. Among those priorities was a blog intended merely to keep friends and family current on my cancer journey. It remains a valued part of my healing process and, in its own way, has afforded me the continued therapeutic benefits of writing. Fans of my particular style of writing have been so generous as to suggest that I write a book. With this effort, I guess we can say I have.

This is not a refined biography of my life, but rather a simple collection of stories told chronologically. Most of what qualifies as embarrassing falls squarely on me. With no desire, however, to further humiliate anyone who associated with me in the past, I've changed the names of people and places in order to offer them some degree of anonymity.

Otherwise, this is how it happened to the best of my recollection, and I hope you'll find it an amusing read. It is ironic, I suppose, that a dreaded diagnosis compels me to share stories that might make some think ill of me. Regardless, I sincerely hope you enjoy this warts-and-all retelling of the funny and fortunate life I've completely enjoyed stumbling through.

AN IRRIGATION DITCH RUNS THROUGH IT

The contributions of desert dwellers to the betterment of mankind are relatively few. They did, however, teach the world some things about water management.

That was hardly an unselfish act. It was simply a matter of self-preservation. In the desert, you either figured out how to manage water efficiently or you shriveled up like crepe paper and blew away in the first summer dust storm.

The pattern of conservation was predictable. First you secured enough water for drinking. Then you set some aside for agriculture, livestock, and light industry. Last, but certainly not least, you figured out how to play in it.

Sure, Hoover Dam slowed the mighty Colorado River to a trickle and created Lake Mead. That massive body of water spun enormous turbines and made Hoover Dam the hydro-electric wonder of the world. Those details were lost, however, on the legions of bass masters and wave crashers who planned their lives around the fishing and water skiing seasons.

This watery wanderlust must be instinctive, because without parental provocation, I was making like a miniature Aquaman before my land skills could take me from riding tricycles to bicycles.

The focus of my aquatic fascination was an irrigation ditch that ran parallel to our property. Its cool waters meandered gently beneath lush, grassy banks and over soft beds of sand. It teamed with wetland wildlife, like desert toads, top minnows, and crawdads—my personal favorite.

My first right of passage was capturing one of those cantankerous crustaceans while steering clear of its death grip. I suppose that sounds like an exaggeration, but the swaying claws of a pissed off crawdad can put a nasty pinch on the tender finger of a five-year-old. Otherwise, the dirt ditch was a haven of harmless fun. That is, of course, unless you shared my capacity for the absurd.

My brothers watched in amazement one afternoon while I, inspired by Jim McKay and waxing poetic about the Acapulco cliff divers on *Wide World of Sports*, executed a near-perfect swan dive into thirteen inches of water. Mom spent the next hour scrubbing sand from my face before putting ice on my first broken nose.

You can imagine our horror when the tide of progress brought our dirt ditch days to an end. One winter, when the ditch saw little use, an army of construction workers swept past our remote homestead and left a cement gorge in their wake. A few weeks later, they released water into the smooth gray "V" that use to be our private water park. Mom studied the rippling current that replaced a once gentle stream and promptly declared it unsafe.

My brothers and I engaged in a collective three-month pout until a warm spring afternoon when the Beckhallers came for a visit.

We didn't really know who the Beckhallers were, but their visit so distracted my parents that my brothers and I were free to move about the family compound unnoticed. We made a beeline for the ditch where Doug, my big brother, suggested I test its waters with a firm shove in the back. I was immediately swept downstream, tumbling end over end. My panic subsided as I got my head above water and extended my feet in front of me. Suddenly, I was butt surfing—and I liked it!

I scrambled up the side of the cement ditch to my excited siblings. In short order, we were hotfooting it down the ditch road a full half-mile north of our house.

We jumped into the recreational rapids one after another, first Doug, then me, then little brother Jeff. We slid down the ditch on our butts for the next hour, winding past our house and traveling another half-mile south before stopping next to the end of our pasture. Then Doug emerged from the water to reveal an image so outrageously unexpected that Jeff and I nearly drowned in our laughter.

The gentle sanding action of the fresh cement surface had completely worn through Doug's cut-off jeans, allowing his dimpled red butt to glow through the seat of his pants like a stoplight. Doug's anger gave way to smug satisfaction as Jeff and I helped each other up and realized we shared our big brother's predicament.

Our only salvation was the alfalfa growing in our pasture adjacent to the ditch. We tucked the leafy stocks in the waistbands of our cut-offs. Together, we fashioned grass skirts that would have made the wardrobe supervisor on *Gilligan's Island* quite proud.

The Beckhallers were on the front porch saying goodbye to my parents as we casually strolled up the long dirt driveway like the Three Stooges in miniature. We stopped at the foot of the porch and looked up, seemingly naked but for the vegetation bunched around our waists. We offered no explanation to the four wide-eyed adults, and they asked for none.

My dad finally broke the silence. "These are my sons," he said. "They're white aborigines." My brothers and I glanced at one another before looking back at the laughing grown-ups. We had no idea what being white aborigines meant, but we liked the sound of it.

Once we were alone again, a few things about our relationship with the high tech ditch became apparent. It was safe, incredibly fun, and would prove to be the most cost effective baby-sitter imaginable. We had yet to fully appreciate, however, just how special our own private water park actually was.

Its clean waters raced down from the higher ground of the Roosevelt Irrigation District to the north with a long, straight, stretch on the north side of the road. That gurgled into a forty-five-foot long tunnel that passed beneath our road and shot you out in front of our property before treating you to a hard left turn and then a bit more straightaway along the front of our property. You then made a fast, sloping decent into the tunnel that ran beneath the narrow bridge that initiated our driveway. Normally, upon exiting that tunnel, we hopped up and ran through a long, wide, shallow section that was too spread out to push our weight; that was fine with us. That area needed to open up to create the pressure necessary to flood the field to the east of our property. The cool thing was, about three times each summer, that section swelled into an eight-foot wide, six-foot deep, thirty-foot long swimming hole that even our parents took advantage of. It fed a right turn through the first waterfall, something we also ran through before hopping butt-ward again for the long, straight slide to the wonder of wonders—the second waterfall.

The man who did the dredging ahead for the cement pour must have noticed our interest in his handy work. He must have also noticed that, although it was getting well into fall, the three young boys who studied him were still berry-brown and sported buzz cuts bleached out by the sun. These were unmistakable signs of a summer spent in the watery environment he was so radically changing. As he dug out what should have been the standard-issue, no-big-deal waterfall nearest our house, he opted to do us an incredible favor. He made us our own private pool. It was easily three times wider, deeper, and longer than the average drop and subsequent whirlpool. The cement guys who followed had to reinforce its sides with four-foot tall by eight-foot long retaining walls that created foot-wide seats for us to sit on. Heck, it was so deep that I could even execute a swan drive from the wood plank bridge across its top without fear of further fracturing my face.

The second waterfall proved so versatile there wasn't much need to go further, but if you rode the nice long straightaway to the end of our property, you encountered the third and last of what we thought of as *our* waterfalls.

Another thing that was glaringly apparent, especially to my mother, was not so wonderful. A single episode in the ditch had rendered three pair of precious cut-off jeans completely worn through and useless, and that would not do.

Mom could harvest a pair of jeans the way a Plain's Indian wasted nothing from a buffalo. What started as crispy new jeans endured a series of patched knees before it became a pair of cut-offs before finally, it went into a hand-me-down cycle. Simply put, what we had just done in an hour of reckless fun was not sustainable in terms of what qualified as our summer swimwear.

Dad's job at the phone company was adequate in most respects, but never seemed to cover all the necessities of a big, growing family, so Mom always had one kind of job or another. Fortunately for us, she happened to be working at the big Goodrich plant to the east when this creative challenge presented itself. Most famous for its tires and blimps, the company also had big military contracts and produced enormous flexible water containment bags it could drop into remote locations to hydrate the troops. Mom worked in that division, and since she was friendly and social as well as industrious, she one day lined up three pair of cut-offs before the gentleman who ran the spray adhesive machine. He laid a thick layer of the black, rubberized sealant across the seats of our otherwise well-worn cut-offs.

Walking toward the ditch in them for the much-anticipated trial run was memorable. First, we looked like some strange tribe of multi-hued baboons sporting conspicuous black bottoms. Second, they were certainly not conducive to dry wear, being crackly and uncomfortable to walk in. But once we hit the water, the magic happened. The saturated jeans seemed to have a softening effect on the adhesive and they flexed with our every move. Suddenly, the problem of the cut-off catastrophe was literally behind us and those black-bottomed cut-offs became the most beautiful attire of our young lives.

I have always been a great fan of the brilliant inventor and statesman, Benjamin Franklin, and while many of his witticisms were clearly repurposed oldies for *Poor Richard's Almanac*, Mom's ingenuity in most all things led me to take one such saying quite literally. I never thought, "Necessity is the mother of invention." I always thought, "If something needs inventing, Mom does it." That's why, somewhere in the dark confines of a remote Arizona desert landfill, there are the still-intact black backsides of otherwise deteriorated cut-off jeans.

As wonderful as our ditch days were, there was one incident that nearly got us expelled from its usually harmless waters, and I inadvertently fueled the drama. We didn't need to be told to never enter a tunnel that was flooded—we knew such tunnels were not only impossible to breath in but also impossible to peer safely through for obstructions. No one wanted to get trapped between a rush of water and debris with only a chest full of air to sort things out.

The problem was that one day the ditch was running hard, and the long tunnel beneath the front road was open on the entry end and concealed with water on the over-full exit end. Since that seemed to explain it, and it had never been blocked before, it proved an attractive nuisance. We pushed our legs into the flooded end as far as we could, but felt no obstructions. If one of us could just confirm the lack of obstructions, we could add an exciting new, hold-your-breath-and-shoot-through dynamic to our watery repertoire.

With Doug and Jeff's nervous approval, I decided to go for it. They looked on at the open end of the tunnel as I hung there with my wet, wrinkled, white knuckles curled over the end of the entry pipe, the rushing water bouncing me in its rapid current. I assured them I would keep my nose up against the top of the pipe and ease in as slowly as I could. I'd grab a chest full of air at the last minute and then slice through however much flooded tunnel remained before meeting them at the other side.

I slipped my fingertips over the edge, pressed them hard against the mossy surface, and eased my way along. So far, so good. My nose was nearly touching the top of the tunnel as the space between it and the water decreased with each soggy second, so I prepared for my all-important last inhale, but then I was shocked into a panicked stop.

Spiders!!! A mass of eerily undulating daddy long-legs spiders collected before my face in a swaying dance of beady bodies and misty limbs in what I was sure was merely a cool escape from the unrelenting heat. But all I could rationalize in that moment was that I wanted to get out. My fingers found their way into a concrete pipe joint seam conveniently located in that section of the tunnel and I dug in and stopped, causing the water to swell around my face and mouth, leaving only my nostrils exposed. I hung there straining to move back against the current that had brought me there, but it was no use. The water was much stronger than I was.

My horrified siblings had no idea this drama was playing out beyond their view, so they were jumping up and down at the other end of the tunnel, anxious for me to emerge.

Ultimately, I didn't actually give up and let go—instead, my exhausted fingers gave way without warning, and I slipped beneath the water without getting an opportunity to pull in that last, all-important gasp of air. Completely submerged, I was spent and breathless as the current alone pulled me along though the cool blackness of the tunnel.

Through closed eyelids, I finally detected the lightness of the tunnel's exit, and that rallied whatever adrenaline I could summon. I shot up through the water and into the air like a trained dolphin hitting its high-flying cue in a water show. I splashed back to safety, but not until Doug was already racing across our long front yard screaming for Mom that "Greg is stuck in the tunnel!"

Obviously, I had some explaining to do, but after a brief banishment and promises of lessons learned, we returned to what proved to be one of the very best aspects of our fortuitous desert upbringing.

CATCHER AND THE WRY

Desert kids never bought into the mystique of "the great American pastime" apparently enjoyed in other regions of the country, nor did we understand why "The Boys of Summer" was a nostalgic euphemism for baseball players.

Our ambivalence toward baseball was due, at least in part, to our weather, which didn't require us to engage in sports on a seasonal basis. There was no threat of coming snow forcing us to compress any particular game into the summer months. We knew only two kinds of weather—winter was hot and summer was dangerously hot. Naturally, we went outside to play in both of our desert seasons.

Left to our own devices—meaning without parental influence—we gravitated to football. For us, football was a beautifully simple game. If you ran faster than kids on the opposing team and crashed into them harder than they crashed into you, you would likely prevail. This was a concept our young, heat-stressed minds could comprehend.

Not so with baseball. It isn't simply that hitting a ball with a bat was one of the hardest things to do in all of sports, but to play the game well, you had to employ strategies that required a high degree of concentration. Maintaining that much focus demanded an attention span greater than that of your average German shepherd. That put us at a distinct disadvantage.

Why, then, would otherwise right-minded adults force children into such a complex sport? There must not be a good answer to that question because the first generation that was subjected to little league baseball came up with T-Ball, a less demanding variation of the grand old game, for their little darlings.

Our poorly-played little league games dragged on unmercifully. Mom gave birth to my sister Janie while waiting for the third out that would bring one such marathon of mediocrity to an acceptable stopping point. We knew we stunk, but it wasn't our fault. We wouldn't have bothered with the game at all had our dads not invested so much time and energy organizing those silly leagues. But what the hell, you got to keep your perspiration-stained cap at the end of the season, and after each game Coach Hatter popped for snow cones.

The emergence of Coach Hatter's son as a gifted pitcher resulted in our one shining season. Umpires loved Louie Hatter. His unique ability to throw the ball relatively near the strike zone meant that games might conclude before the score ran as high as the temperature. But Louie's pitching was just one of the keys to our success that season. The other was Coach Hatter's revolutionary "Big Catcher Strategy."

Before Coach Hatter changed the look of our little league forever, catchers were usually little guys who could scramble quickly to the backstop. That might prevent a fleet-footed base runner from stretching a wild pitch into a two-base error. Then came Buddy Jackson, the biggest kid in two counties. Even Louie's most errant curve ball was likely to plow deep into Buddy's chest protector and fall harmlessly in front of him with a dull thud.

I can't remember every kid who played on our team that summer, but I will always remember Buddy Jackson. I know Matt Stevens will forever try to forget him.

Buddy Jackson and Matt Stevens could not have been more different from one another. Buddy was huge in an environment that was exceedingly unkind to people of considerable girth. Even during the coolest months, Buddy's upper lip sported a mustache of beaded perspiration. And during the hot months, he was the last kid you wanted to sit next to on a crowded school bus. Not that Buddy was any more or less hygienic than other kids. Most of us entered a bathtub only at gunpoint. It's just that sitting next to the perpetually perspiring Buddy was always an uncomfortably moist experience.

Matt Stevens, on the other hand, always looked as though he stepped from the pages of the Sears catalogue—the dreaded publication which featured ill-fitting jeans in navy, rust, and avocado. Every August my mom dutifully ordered those ugly pants, signaling the end of summer fun.

One game day before the awful jeans arrived, our winning streak was on the line. The ever-pristine Matt Stevens had just performed the pre-game ritual of emptying the equipment bag in front of the dugout. He was kicking the pile of gear into an accessible spread when something caught his attention. Reaching past the face mask, shin guards, and chest protector that transformed Buddy into a knight in dusty armor, Matt picked up a pear-shaped piece of gray plastic vented with six prominent air holes. He drew it near his face for closer examination, cocking his head to one side like a curious puppy. Then Matt did the unthinkable, he pressed the item firmly over his nose and mouth and asked in a pitifully muted voice, "What's this for?"

Matt was the only one in the ballpark unaware that he was drawing air through Buddy Jackson's rancorous crotch protector.

The team reacted instantly and in unison. We fell to the ground as surely as if an unhappy postal worker had sprayed the diamond with automatic weapon fire. Yet things were strangely quiet, for we were experiencing that rarest form of laughter—the silent scream variety.

We never quite recovered. Our hitting, fielding, and Louie's usually reliable pitching were infected with an unrelenting case of the giggles. Even stoic Coach Hatter was reduced to silliness. Normally a pillar of reserve in the first base coaching box, he intermittently turned his back on the infield in a valiant attempt to hide his laughter and spare Matt further humiliation. Yet on each occasion, his laughter was given away by the bobbing of this skinny shoulders.

It was our only loss of the season, but no one ever complained about it.

Those of us on the team wondered how Matt would possibly survive the torment that surely awaited him when school resumed in September. We never found out. His family moved quietly away later that summer.

Over the years, I came to realize what a compassionate man Matt's father must have been. He realized there were certain indignities in life a boy should not have to endure—in Matt's case, living down that moment with Buddy Jackson's crotch protector on his face was one of them.

THE BEST ALBUM EVER

I stood frozen at Fed-Mart's magazine rack. The forerunner to stores like Wal-Mart and Costco, Fed-Mart offered just about everything you could think of under one roof. With their young family growing out of control, my parents needed just about everything you could think of on a fairly regular basis. This resulted in twice-monthly marathon visits to Fed-Mart, giving my brothers and me ample time to explore its many wonders.

On this particular day, I was indulging my growing fascination with print media at Fed-Mart's generous magazine rack. I held open before me the latest issue of *MAD* magazine. My eyes, however, were elsewhere. I tested the limits of my peripheral vision to determine if anyone was looking my way. When the coast was clear, I nonchalantly slid the new issue of *Playboy* between the pages of my *MAD* magazine façade. Anyone looking my way would assume that I was grinning at the comic stylings of Jack Davis, when in fact, the tatas on Miss April were the true source of my amusement.

Just then, someone came up behind me and asked, "What are you doing?" Startled, I looked up to see my older brother, Doug. He was the one who taught me the *MAD/Playboy* maneuver in the first place.

"Trying not to pee my pants," I responded.

Doug looked down at the *MAD* magazine I was holding and asked, "So, how are things in the land of stupid?"

"What now?" I asked defensively, only then realizing I was holding the magazine upside down. As I started to turn it right side up, Doug commanded, "Put that down and come with me."

I began to protest, but Doug interrupted, "Forget it. We can check it out next time we're at Grandmas." He was right. Not that my Grandma subscribed to or had even seen a *Playboy* magazine, but Uncle Bobby had. The last of her live-at-home brood, Uncle Bobby had converted the storage shed behind Grandma's house into a makeshift workout and weight-lifting room. Miss April would, no doubt, join the gallery of centerfolds that adorned its walls.

I hurried to keep up with Doug, his beige cowboy boots thumping along Fed-Mart's glistening, green, asbestos tile flooring. I expected him to make the usual turn at the toy section to look at models, but instead, he kept going. When I caught up to him, he was standing in the store's music section holding a record album in his hands. As I approached, he said almost reverently, "This is the best album ever." He continued, "*The Greatest Hits of The Beatles*. All their best stuff and none of the other stuff."

Only half interested, I scanned the enormity of the music department before asking "You gonna ask Mom and Dad to buy it?"

"Don't be stupid," Doug responded sharply. I rarely took offense to being called stupid, because I never assumed Doug was suggesting I was any stupider than any other eleven-year-old. Being younger, I could not help but say things that would sound stupid to a thirteen-year-old. Besides, given the lengths my parents went to stretch their budget in order to cover the necessities, it *was* rather stupid to think they would entertain buying a record album for Doug.

Then Doug got my undivided attention. "I'm going to buy it," he said. I leaned in closer and looked at the big red price tag in the upper right corner of the album. It read $2.98. That was a weeks' worth of bathroom-scrubbing-trash-hauling-weed-chopping allowance.

"You sure?" I asked. "You could buy a couple of models for that much money."

"I knew you wouldn't get it," Doug replied. "You're too little."

"I get it," I shot back. "These are all the songs the high school kids sing on the bus." So spread out were the houses in the remote area where we grew up that our elementary school and the nearest high school coordinated collecting kids from the far corners of the district. As a result, we often rode the bus with much older kids. Its radio was tuned to an AM rocker with an unrelenting, Beatles-heavy playlist. Then it occurred to me that Doug was on the threshold of being a high school kid himself, and he was standing there convincing himself that he should make a teenage-type purchase.

"I am going to buy it," he repeated. Then he added, "of course, you'll get to listen to it, too."

I liked the sound of that and leaned in closer. I wanted to say something supportive, but instead I said the first thing that came to mind. "That's a funny-looking guitar!"

"It's British, stupid. It even has a British flag painted on it." He went on, "They're from Liverpool, ya know."

I didn't know. I wrinkled up my nose and said, "I don't much like liver."

"Forget it," he said. Then he tucked the album under his arm and started for the front of the store.

"Where ya going?" I asked. "To buy this," he responded. I called after him, "But don't you want to wait until Mom and Dad check out?" There was no response. "As long as we're here, ya wanna look at the models?" I asked that even louder to compensate for the growing distance between us, but he was already on the next aisle headed toward the cashiers.

I went ahead and visited the toy department and checked out the new model cars and trucks. Sure enough, there were some cool ones. At least, I was pretty sure they were cool. Doug would have known for sure.

Making my way along the rows of crowded checkout stands, I watched for Doug but did not see him in any of the lines. I finally reached a stand that was closed and ducked under the chain intended to keep people from cutting through. At the very front of the store in the exit area beyond the cashiers, I found Doug sitting on a small bench, framed nicely by a chrome trash can and a wall-mounted fire extinguisher.

I plopped down beside him. "All yours?" I asked.

"Yep," he said, "and I can't wait to get it home."

But wait he would. Fed-Mart was located on 19th Avenue in what was then considered west Phoenix. Our house was out past Cotton Tail Road, which was roughly the equivalent of 195th Avenue. Doug endured half a dozen traffic signals and even more stop signs before we reached the rural expanse that would allow Dad to maintain a cruising speed Doug found acceptable.

Our car had barely stopped rolling up the driveway when Doug, album firmly in hand, bolted from the car and into the house. Under the circumstances, he was not required to carry in two bags of groceries like the rest of us. By the time I dropped my load of groceries on the kitchen table, Doug was already lowering the arm of our record player onto the first cut of the best album ever. Within seconds, our living room was filled with the sound of an entire violin section offering a flowery introduction to "Love Me Do."

Doug stiffened and stared at the record player. As I walked into the living room and picked up the album cover, he was anxiously moving the record player's arm to the shiny line that separated the first cut from the second. Cut two began with an army of kettledrums failing to capture the energy needed for a convincing rendition of "She Loves You."

Examining the album cover, I shook my head and repeated, "That's a funny-looking guitar." By that time, my Dad was looking at the cover, too. From over my shoulder he corrected me, "That's not a guitar, it's a cello."

Doug turned and yanked the album cover from my hands and somehow, for the first time, noticed the not-so-fine-print above the words *The Greatest Hits of The Beatles.*" There it read, "The London Philharmonic presents…"

The only thing that spared us from the sad droning of an oboe solo was my sudden explosion of laughter. Though I would soon regret it, the laughter was genuine, as I found the whole scenario truly hilarious. There was, however, a little extra glee in my squeals at finally having some company in "the land of stupid."

Through squinted eyes from a face contorted with laughter, I watched Doug redden to a shade I would come to know in high school art class as vermilion. I coaxed my arms up from my aching sides to protect either side of my face, certain that a series of head kicks was in my immediate future. Those kicks never came. Instead, he turned on the heels of his beige cowboy boots and raced from the room. By the time I got to the window, Doug was already at the end of our long dirt driveway. Being bigger and stronger than his bullied younger siblings, Doug was less accustomed to hotfooting it out the front door than we were. Yet, by most any standard, he made good time. He disappeared into the cotton field across the road while we listened to a strangely downtempo version of "I Feel Fine."

I walked around the fields that surrounded our house quite often, daydreaming or trying to sort out things that confused me. Doug went there less frequently, and when he did it was usually to conceal his utter rage or abject disappointment. The longer he stayed away, the more I realized he was struggling with both.

When he finally returned to the house, I looked forward to the beating that would relieve my guilt for having laughed at him and thereby restore me to the more comfortable role of victim. But it did not happen. Instead, Doug walked past me with all the dignity he could muster and calmly buried the instrumental version of the *Greatest Hits of The Beatles* in the middle of Mom and Dad's modest record collection. It remained there until a spunky retiree discovered it at the big church rummage sale a few years later.

We did not speak of the album incident for a long, long time. Fortunately, it did not put Doug off buying records. He did, however, opt for comedy albums more times than not. First it was Cosby, then Carlin, and then Pryor. And in every case, I got to listen to them, too.

It would be more than three decades before they would actually release the best album ever—or I should say, the best CD ever. As soon as I learned about The Beatles *1*, a collection of their twenty-seven number one hits, I rushed out to buy it for my brother. Not that it was necessary from a fence-mending point of view. No, our relationship endured this and other wonder year traumas quite nicely.

In fact, we still have as much fun together as the realities of adult life allow. We even end up in the toy section of a department store every once in a while, looking at models. I can still count on Doug to pick out the really cool ones.

FREE STYLE SCOUTING

I decided to step down as senior patrol leader of Mercury Boy Scout Troop 39 even before Conrad Givens took the Williams brothers hostage on our camp out to McClousky Dam. It's not as though the troop had completely descended into darkness, like Colonel Kurtz' renegade Marines in *Apocalypse Now*. No, instead we hovered in a gray area between that and the groupthink of *Lord of The Flies*.

It had not always been that way. In fact, just a few years before, Troop 39 was exemplary in every way. My decision to leave the Boy Scouts after three short years was because I sensed that the completely unstructured fun we started to have was a disaster waiting to happen.

Many of the skills one learns as a Scout fade over time. Tying clove hitches or signaling someone on a distant hilltop with semaphore flags just doesn't come up enough in everyday life to keep those skills sharp. But what I learned about leadership from Scouting has stayed with me ever since.

Troop 39 was enjoying its glory days just as I joined its ranks. For a small, rural area, Mercury boasted a robust group of boys with more than its share of Star, Life, and Eagle Scouts. Most of the credit for our troop's success rested squarely on our Scoutmaster, CT Lawton, who just happened to be my uncle.

Uncle CT was a no-nonsense, dust-bowl refugee who had relocated to a modest desert burb most others had the good sense to simply pass through. I suspect my Mom's lovely older sister, Aunt Ruth, was the reason he settled down in Mercury. From the humblest of beginnings, Uncle CT graduated college, entered the field of public school administration, and worked his way up to principal of Mercury Elementary.

CT was a capable and confident person, and he expected the same of his Scouts. They responded in kind by studying hard and ripping through various rank and merit badge requirements in workman like fashion. Efficiently meeting the required aspects of Scouting left plenty of time for what might be described as electives, and those were best displayed on camp outs.

Even Uncle CT's by-the-book, almost military mentality went off the rails on camp outs. Perhaps that's because "the book," which was, in this case, the all-important *Boy Scout Handbook*, had not yet caught up with the fact that some adventuresome pilgrims were settling in America's desert southwest. The illustrated *Boy Scout Handbook* offered images of shimmering lakes, bucolic hill sides, and towering pines. We, however, camped out where what passed for vegetation sported thorns, where reptiles and insects competed to see which could be the most lethally venomous, and where afternoon temperatures were perilous for the unprepared. This required Uncle CT to adapt generic Scouting principals to the reality of our desert landscape. And that wee bit of latitude was the only spark he needed to ignite the Jekyll and Hyde aspects of his personality.

CT Lawton played as outrageously in the field as he worked in the classroom. We were usually carted out to the desert in the school's World War II surplus Power Wagon. Once safely off-road, Uncle CT would lock in the hubs and exploit the vintage four-wheel drive in ways his young charges found delightfully unsafe.

Some Scoutmasters might use a discarded car hood in the desert as an opportunity for a life lesson. Perhaps they would take it to a proper landfill or recycling center. Not CT Lawton. When we found an old car hood, he flipped it upside down, lashed it to the bumper of the Power Wagon, loaded it up with Scouts, and took us pounding over rocks and through dry river beds. A half-dozen of us started out balancing like big wave surfers; we bounced off one by one until one lone kid was left balancing on the mangled, inverted hood and could claim bragging rights. The runners-up provided lots of hands-on opportunities for those Scouts working on first-aid merit badges.

If CT's idea of spontaneous recreation was scary, some of his structured efforts were even worse. Each summer, he chose a desert camp out event for the initiation of new Scouts. Initiation camp outs were always well attended because any Scout who had already endured one wanted their chance to do unto others as had been done unto him. These ceremonies always took place in a dry, sandy river bed because they were hard to run in. In deep, soft sand, two-thirds of the energy intended to propel you forward was lost as your shoes churned into the soft mushiness beneath your feet. This made a dry river bed the perfect setting for a belt line.

Belt lines were beautifully simple. The more senior Scouts formed two lines facing one another. The uninitiated then charged between them while whirling belts painfully whipped the initiates with each frantic stride. The pain endured by the lowly Tenderfoot scouts was equaled only by the delight of the belt-wielding veteran scouts. So cool was Mercury Boy Scout Troop 39 that we all gladly endured this torture in order to finally be counted among its ranks. Then, it all changed.

One day, CT Lawton resigned as Scoutmaster. The reason he gave was that his promotion to superintendent of our grade school didn't leave him enough time for Scouting, but I knew the real reason. Like my dad had, Uncle CT bought a small piece of property in the mountains of central Arizona, and now all his free time was dedicated to building a cabin. I suspect there was another reason, too. While things in the late 1960s weren't nearly as litigious as they would become in the decades that followed, CT seemed to know his approach to Scouting was going out of style. Today, of course, attorneys and child protective service agents would be picking over his bones. I suppose concealing our belt line welts was the ultimate expression of support, and it might have kept him with our troop even longer than he intended.

Enter Hamilton Knowles. We *knew* Uncle CT had trouble keeping his inner child in check, but with Ham Knowles, we had to wonder if he had ever actually *been* a child. Many argued that he was born a forty-year-old. If he had been a kid, he was no doubt a Boy Scout of the goody-two-shoes, straight-arrow variety. That was okay with me. The highlight of my only camp out under CT had been the belt line initiation, so I welcomed Mr. Knowles with a bruised butt and an open mind.

Hamilton Knowles taught eighth grade at Mercury Elementary, and the regular Scout meetings seemed like an extension of his classroom. The troop continued to meet the rank and merit badge requirements efficiently, but his approach to camp outs was purely academic. This was the only excuse the oldest boys needed to finally drop out of Boy Scouts. As guys old enough to drive themselves to high school, they had stayed on out of loyalty to CT, but with him gone and Mr. Knowles showing no interest in reckless fun, they bailed in short order.

The next oldest group of boys, the thirteen- and fourteen-year-olds, decided to wait and see if the uptight Mr. Knowles loosened up. This group included my big brother, Doug, and the always serious Willy Post. I know they genuinely missed CT, but I suspect the more even-keeled style of Mr. Knowles offered them, and us younger Scouts, a good opportunity to recalibrate.

On our first camp out with Mr. Knowles, I learned that I would have rather endured a violent desert thunderstorm than to camp in close quarters with Shane Marks. It wasn't that I disliked Shane; in fact, we sometimes rode the four-mile distance between our houses for an afternoon of goofing off together. But Shane was a strong personality, and spending a few finite hours playing with him was very different than having him in your immediate space for an entire weekend, particularly if the weekend meant sharing a tent with him. His last minute request to join the troop on one particular camp out meant just that, so the bigger-than-life Shane Marks became the fourth camper in a tent intended for only three.

The three entitled to the tent included myself, my younger cousin Joey (who was Uncle CT's son), and our friend Ozzie Denning. Traveling and setting up camp always makes for a long first day and, at the end of that one, we were ready for sleep. Even if Shane's body was tired, his mouth had never experienced fatigue, so while the rest of us lay in our sleeping bags, he was still up, chatting and screwing around.

Although Joey would eventually grow up to tower over me, at the time, he was the smallest of us. As such, we tucked him tightly into the side of the tent where one of its 45-degree walls met the ground. I wedged in between Joey and Ozzie, and that left Shane to occupy the other side of the tent. As his immediate neighbor, Ozzie took most of the bumps and nudges as Shane continued to bustle about.

"Geez, Shane, when are you going to get into your sleeping bag?" Ozzie asked.

"I can't," Shane explained. "I gotta go pee."

"Well," Ozzie responded, "you know where the latrine is, get on with it."

"I'm not going out there!" Shane exclaimed.

"Pee. Don't pee. I don't care. Just knock it off so we can get some sleep," Ozzie said as he joined Joey and me in closing his eyes.

It was finally quiet. Perhaps Ozzie thought it was too quiet because he opened his eyes, located Shane, and let out a loud sigh. This prompted me and Joey to open our eyes, too. That's when we saw Shane on his knees, facing away from us, his jeans loosened, and his hips pressed to the front of our tent.

"What the hell are you doing?" Ozzie demanded.

Shane twisted his head in order to look back over his shoulder and asked, "What does it look like I'm doing?"

"Humping the tent," replied Ozzie, "but I'll bet you just pissed on our entryway, you butthead."

"It'll dry," Shane shrugged.

We closed our eyes again, thinking Shane was finally ready to turn in, but after just a few more precious moments of quiet, an increasingly exasperated Ozzie bellowed at Shane once more. "Holy shit, Shane! What are you doing now?"

Joey and I again looked over. This time we saw Shane doing what looked like a poorly executed, one-handed pushup. His feet were spread too far apart, his butt was too high in the air, and his free hand seemed to be smoothing out the corners of his sleeping bag. What was most striking about this pose, however, was that Shane was completely naked. "Chill out, Ozzie," Shane dead-panned, "I'm just fixing my bed roll."

"But why are you bare-assed?" pressed Ozzie.

"Why not? I sleep in the raw at home, why shouldn't I do it here?"

"Because at home your ugly ass isn't within spitting distance of my face!" complained Ozzie.

At that point I chimed in with "Boom, boom, boom, boom…" and recognizing the tune, Joey decided to accompany me, "I see your hiney, it's white and shiny, if you don't hide it, I'm gonna bite it..."

We all began to laugh—we laughed so loudly that it was impossible to hear the approach of Mr. Knowles until his face and flashlight were peering into the front of our tent with Shane still assuming a most unflattering pose. Our sophisticated naturalist then spun around, slamming his bare butt onto the tent's gritty floor while clutching his shiny blue sleeping bag to his chest in a fit of newfound modesty.

"What's going on here?" Mr. Knowles demanded. I suppose his question was directed to all of us, but Mr. Knowles knew us well enough to suspect that Shane should be the focus of his attention.

When no one offered an explanation, he began to scold us. Well, technically he was scolding us, but Mr. Knowles was so soft-spoken that it came off more like one of his classroom lectures—a lecture that focused on our growing bodies and their absolute need for a good night's sleep. He went on to note that if we weren't mature enough to recognize our own needs, we should at least show some consideration to our fellow Scouts who did. By the time Mr. Knowles' tongue lashing concluded, Joey had been lured into a deep sleep, and I was feeling awfully drowsy myself.

Just as Mr. Knowles prepared to leave, he looked down at the damp ground where he had been kneeling and asked, "What is the source of this moisture?" As his flashlight once again illuminated the interior of our tent, Ozzie and I instinctively jerked our heads in Shane's direction.

"Uh...ah...well...I emptied my canteen out there," he eventually stammered.

"You shouldn't have emptied right in front of your tent," Mr. Knowles said tersely. And with that, he withdrew, but he could not have been out of earshot before we burst into laughter one last time.

Sure, Shane had lied, and poorly at that. But his absurd explanation altered the vernacular for the balance of that camp out. From that point on, no one "went pee," or "took a whizz." Instead, we "emptied our canteens."

To his credit, Mr. Knowles took this kind of nonsense in stride. Had there been a wise-ass merit badge, I would have met the requirements in a heartbeat, and this is why I liked Mr.

Knowles. If you paid attention, you could see that he had a dry sense and humor and a subtly sarcastic wit. My eighteen months under his tutelage were enlightening and entertaining, and I made the rank of First Class Scout in relatively short order.

Then, just as CT had stepped down when promoted from principal to superintendent, so too did Hamilton Knowles when promoted from eighth grade teacher to principal.

Once again, the troop was thrown into limbo while we awaited new adult supervision. My dad would have made a wonderful Scoutmaster. He was not as industrious as Uncle CT, nor as focused as Mr. Knowles, but he was just as capable where it really counted. He was laid back and had a great sense of humor that would have been a hit with the guys. But Dad had already paid his dues with 4H and our church, and like Uncle CT, he was working on a cabin of his own. But we didn't remain without a Scoutmaster for long.

THE CATCH

Mercury Elementary School once again became our source for a new Scoutmaster, and this time it came in the form of a young bachelor and sixth grade teacher named Vic Valance. Perhaps he noticed how the previous Scoutmasters had ascended to the highest ranks of the school's administration and thought the job must be an incubator for some essential skill sets. Or, perhaps he was just a supreme suck-up, but either way he was about to embark on a job for which he was completely ill-equipped.

As our regular Scout meetings once again adjusted to the leadership style of a new Scoutmaster, it was painfully clear that Mr. Valance had never been a Scout as a boy and never expected to be a Scoutmaster as an adult. But the real void in leadership didn't become apparent until he joined us for his first desert camp out. Thank goodness Dad agreed to come along. My big brother Doug and I convinced Dad that Mr. Valance couldn't find the desert that laid just beyond a few miles of the cotton fields, let alone a good camp site, so Dad took the weekend off to guide us into *el tierra en fuego*.

We set off Friday after school. Once we arrived, my dad focused on finding a good camp site and setting up the chuck wagon. Mr. Valance should have been available for official Scoutmasterly duties, but he didn't have the vaguest idea how to do that. As experienced little campers, we simply went about setting up our individual camps and preparing our dinners. Uncle CT and Mr. Knowles had shown us how to dig a hole in the ground and fill it with rocks before building a fire on top of it. Once the fire burned down to coals, we would brush them away and place corn, potatoes, carrots, and a hunk of meat over the blistering hot stones. Then we would place a damp piece of burlap over the food before covering it all up with dirt. In a couple of hours, our efforts resulted in the mini-equivalent of a Hawaiian luau. We could all do this as casually as throwing a frozen dinner in the oven. Not so with Mr. Valance. He had actually brought frozen dinners and had them on bent sticks perched precariously above an open campfire. The remaining older Scouts where evaluating Mr. Valance's every move, and so far they weren't impressed.

The next day, things got even worse. Mr. Knowles always had some organized activity, followed by rank and merit badge evaluations. With him gone, none of those things happened, so we all just went about entertaining ourselves. Individual and small group interests were pretty much exhausted by late afternoon, so we all ended up in the dry river bed for a game of football.

Like my brother Doug, Willy Post was one of those fourteen-year-olds trying to decide whether to remain in the troop or not. He directed a group of us younger Scouts to clear the rocks away from a nice, shallow section of the dry river bed next to our camp site. Someone had brought one of those cheap, smaller-than-regulation footballs that are easy for young hands to throw. The game was on. We played full contact tackle football in the sand for a well over an hour before my dad called us to come and help with the evening's group dinner preparations.

Since we were already in the huddle when Dad summoned us, it was understood that the next play would be our last. I was on Willy's team and wasn't at all surprised when he said that he would throw a Hail Mary pass. What did surprise me was his decision that I would be his primary target. For most of the game, he had thrown to boys who were bigger and, most importantly, older than me. Those older boys were not any faster than me, however, and Willy had noticed that I was often open.

We broke huddle and I lined up on the far right side opposite another younger Scout, Santiago Macias. Santiago was pretty quick himself, but given the lack of action we had seen that afternoon, he wasn't expecting a play to come our way. The ball was snapped to Willy and I faked left as I'd done a dozen times already, but then broke right with much more energy than Santiago expected. By the time he realized the pass was intended for me, I was already by him. Willy saw this too, and the combination of an open target and the last play of the game supercharged his arm with adrenalin.

As he hurled the ball skyward, I was not worried about Santiago defending the pass since I was already several yards past him. The real question was whether I would be able to catch up to the ball. Just as I was about to concede that my best effort would not allow me to reach the football's landing spot, an unexpected thing happened—my feet emerged from the sandy riverbed and found solid ground. Feeling my well-worn Keds gain speed on the hard, sun-baked desert surface instead of the soft sand gave me hope. The excitement of this realization infused my sprint with the same gusto Willy clearly felt when he launched his pass.

Along with my fear that I wouldn't be able to get to the ball in time, another question caused me to doubt my efforts—was I out of bounds? Thus far the game had been played entirely within the confines of the dry river bed. Technically, however, no one had defined the sidelines, but only an idiot would have left the soft, sandy surface of the wash for the host of hazards on the open desert floor. My take on this issue was unimportant anyway, as the older Scouts would undoubtedly be the ones to argue it out. The point was moot, however, unless I caught up to the ball.

And catching up was exactly what I was doing. My path was determined entirely by the trajectory of Willy's pass. My eyes remained fixed on the ball and I was increasingly confident that I had a legitimate shot at catching it. Time for another question—should I dive for it? No, of course not! The pea-sized bits of quartz and granite that littered the desert floor would make me feel like an ant skidding across a sheet of course sand paper.

Suddenly, the decision was taken out of my hands, or perhaps I should say my feet, as my left toe slammed squarely into a rock jutting up from the desert runway that was, up to that point, surprisingly clear. I should have been horrified at the prospect of skidding to a stop on such an inhospitable surface, but in that fraction of a second, with my eyes still trained on the ball, I was instead emboldened with visions of glory. I realized I still had a very good chance of making the catch, and that would salve the nasty abrasions that surely awaited my elbows.

BAM! Then everything went black and I was confronted with a new question—what the heck just happened? My eyes were instinctively slammed shut and it took me a moment to realize I had hit something—something big and solid enough to bring me to a dead stop. In the two seconds it took before I opened my eyes, a surprising number of thoughts raced through my mind. I wasn't in any pain, but the body's ability to instantly anesthetize itself when necessary is quite remarkable. I was completely conscious, however, so pain or no pain, I had been spared from diving headlong into a Palo Verde tree, or God forbid, a rock hard Mesquite tree. I must have gotten lucky. It was probably a big Greasewood, those tough but airy-looking bushes whose small waxy leaves cover the ends of their rangy gray branches.

I eased my eyes open. It took another moment for them to find some depth perception between whatever had stopped me and the reddish dirt of the ground just beyond it.

Thorns! Holy crap! Big, ugly thorns!

As I slowly extracted myself from its branches, the Staghorn cactus I landed in came into focus. This was a big one, about three feet tall and almost as wide at its top. The cactus was so named because its arms resemble the slightly irregular V-shape of a male mule deer's antlers.

Pushing back onto my knees, I looked down to see an abundance of broken, dark gray thorns generously deposited across my hands and forearms. It hadn't occurred to me yet that the pattern continued up across my shoulders and to my neck. As I steadied myself enough to stand, I heard the pounding of footsteps as the other Scouts raced up behind me.

I slowly turned to face them, they stopped in their tracks, and I watched the little swirls of dust settle about their feet. If the gravity of the situation hadn't yet hit me, the horrified looks on their faces went a long way toward getting me there. As the others stood paralyzed, my brother Doug stepped toward me.

"Don't...touch...me," I hissed though clinched teeth. "Don't...touch...me."

I didn't clinch my teeth and hiss out of pain, and it wasn't shock—it was simply a practical matter. If you hit certain types of cactus, like Staghorn, Cholla, or Prickly Pear hard enough, they will break at the point where their joints come together. I had smacked this particular Staghorn cactus quite hard, and it had responded by embedding one of its joints in the left side of the back of my head. Another joint was in the front right side of my neck. Finally, a third joint was in the left side of my face, half its needles in my upper lip, the other half bridging to my lower lip, hence I had no choice but to hiss through clinched teeth.

With my arms extended out from my body like a zombie, I slowly staggered up a small hill to the spot where my dad and Mr. Valance had set up their section of the camp. My dad was the only person who seemed to take the insanity of the scene in stride, but then again, he had lots of practice.

I know that each of my siblings connected with our parents in their own unique way. But I connected with Dad through injuries. Owing to my inflated sense of athleticism and a conspicuous lack of judgment, I was the kid that Dad patched up with alarming regularity. There had already been numerous occasions during which he had lifted me onto the dining room table and cracked open the institutional green first-aid kit that he decided was surplus from one of his many telephone company repair trucks.

On this particular evening, in addition to that first-aid kit, my accident *du jour* required that Dad also get out his tool box and sanitize a pair of long-nosed pliers. He used them for the next forty-five minutes. He plucked and I winced while Mr. Valance looked on in stunned silence. Dad had to meticulously move from thorn to thorn, coaxing the little barbed spears from my flesh before swabbing the remaining wound with alcohol. While I tried to focus more on the sunset than on my pain, I noticed something that I couldn't believe I missed earlier. There in the distance was the cactus I crashed into, cradling the little deflated football I had been so determined to catch. I found out later that one of the boys went to retrieve it but Willy Post stopped him. He ordered it to remain there as a monument to "the catch that almost was."

If Mr. Valance had any thoughts of a long tenure as our Scoutmaster, they vanished with my Cirque du Scary performance with the cactus. Frankly, no one was sorry to see him go, but the idea of once again adjusting to new leadership was the last straw for Doug, Willy, and the other older boys in the troop. They quit, and all that remained of Mercury Boy Scout Troop 39 was a handful of eleven- and twelve-year-olds in search of even a modicum of adult supervision. And finally, a modicum of adult supervision is exactly what we got, but it took a while to arrive.

With no Scoutmaster in the offing, we found other things to do with the nights that were previously devoted to our regular meetings. The school year was almost over by the time Robbie Jamison came running up to me, too excited to stand still and shouted, "He said he'd do it! My dad's going to be our Scoutmaster!"

I could tell Robbie wanted me to clutch his hands so we could jump up and down like ecstatic little girls, but I just stood there looking at him. I was reasonably familiar with Robbie's dad, and it was hard to imagine a more unlikely person to invest time in the nurturing of young boys. In fact, it was hard to imagine Bob Jamison anywhere in the American Southwest.

At about five foot and three inches tall, Mr. Jamison wasn't even as big as some of us kids. He wore black, horn-rimmed glasses, and the hair that survived his receding hair line was long, black, and loopy. It was much easier to imagine him in his former environment as a jazz percussionist in the biggest cities—New York, Detroit, and Chicago. He fell in love and started a family later in life than most men of that era, but he made up for lost time with Mrs. Jamison by cranking out six kids in rapid succession. Their oldest child was my friend and classmate, Robbie. The realities of family life required a day job, and as things worked out, that day job caused the Jamisons to migrate to Arizona. Mr. Jamison was a fish out of water, and a fish can't get any more out of water than getting deposited in the middle of a vast desert—but there he was.

As quiet and introverted as he was diminutive, bringing home the bacon seemed to be the limit of his responsibilities to his family. His tall, gregarious wife ran the household and tried to compensate for his almost crippling shyness.

That is why I couldn't find words to respond to Robbie's shocking declaration. At first I just shrugged and thought to myself that beggars can't be choosers. Besides, we younger Scouts were not as jaded or picky as the older boys who recently defected. But then I thought further about Robbie's well-developed powers of persuasion. I could just hear him assuring his dad that all he would be required to do was show up and unlock the door to the tiny, retired auditorium that Mercury Elementary School reserved for the Boy Scouts to use. Mr. Jamison probably heard that and took Robbie at his word because showing up to unlock the door is what he did—only that and nothing more.

During our first meeting with our new Scoutmaster, we flooded the Scout room with our diminished ranks, and Mr. Jamison found his way to the quietest corner of the room where he read a book for a while then put his feet up on the small but right-sized for him furniture and took a nap. This isn't what we were used to, but at least Mr. Jamison showed up for us and that was more than any other adult seemed willing to do.

Without Mr. Knowles, our tight ship had sunk some time ago. Mr. Valance was a dud, but the older Scouts compensated. With neither option available to us, we stood in a circle and looked at one another. Finally, Robbie broke the silence by asking, "Okay, Greg, what now?"

I didn't retreat from the question, but I didn't answer right away either. After thinking for a minute I said, "How about this? We see if anyone wants help with Boy Scout stuff. If not, we work on a skit, and after that we go outside for some British Bulldog."

The group flashed gap-toothed grins, gave each other self-congratulatory slaps on the back, and verbalized various statements to the affirmative. The fact was that there was absolutely nothing unique in what I had proposed. It was exactly what we did during the most disciplined days under Mr. Knowles, but it was all a matter of proportions.

Mr. Knowles had us spend 75% of each meeting working on the priority skill sets in the *Boy Scout Handbook*. With the other 25%, we alternated between performing skits on the little stage that occupied half the Scout room's footprint, or playing British

Bulldog, a man-in-the-middle tackle game that kids loved and parents hated because of the toll it took on our clothing.

Naturally, during our first meeting as a complete democracy, we spent the first half of our time doing skits and the other half playing outside. We remained drunk with freedom and where equally undisciplined at the next meeting, but by the third, we were actually eager to act like Scouts again and started addressing the three areas of importance in equal proportions. We only spent one-third of our time on advancing our Scouting prowess, and while that may not sound like much, it proved vitally important. Without the previous sophisticated adult leadership, or role-modeling from more experienced boys, we had to figure things out for ourselves. As a result, I believe we bonded as a team in ways that few boys, Scouts or otherwise, ever get to.

I didn't really consider the idea that Robbie's deference to me without protest from the other boys was a vote of confidence. Of the eight kids in the troop, about half were eleven and the rest of us were twelve. I was not the oldest, nor the smartest, but I was probably as athletic as any of the boys. But I think what most impressed them about me went back to my pursuit of Willy Post's errant pass. I never had to tell the story because Ozzie, Robbie, and Santiago were always happy to share it. And they, after all, had a better view of the event than I did. I began to notice that the story got a little more fantastic with each retelling, but the way it concluded was always the same: "and he didn't even cry." I guess the credibility quotient on that aspect of the adventure was pretty important to boys our age because it gave me a lot of credibility.

THE RELUCTANT LEADER

As much as I appreciated the support of my friends in the troop, my leadership position was further galvanized when the regional headquarters for the Boy Scouts was finally able to connect with Mr. Jamison. They had a program called Junior Leadership Camp Training intended to help senior patrol leaders with—well—leadership. I was anything but senior and I'm not sure I even qualified as our patrol leader yet, but Mr. Jamison let me know that I was chosen to represent our troop. I'll never know if Robbie or

Mr. Knowles influenced Mr. Jamison, or if he arrived at the decision himself, but the appeal to my ego just slightly outweighed my trepidation.

Going by the acronym of JLCT, Junior Leadership Camp Training took place the week immediately prior to Troop 39's regular summer slot at Camp Geronimo, the main Boy Scout camp in the cool pine forests of central Arizona. That meant I would be away from home for two weeks compared to everyone else's one week away.

At JLCT, I learned some Boy Scout history. William Boyce was a Chicago businessman who visited London in 1909. There he was afforded a good deed by a lad who was later immortalized as the "Unknown Boy Scout." So impressed was Mr. Boyce that the following year he imported the Boy Scout program from England to the United States. Since then, the American Boy Scout organization has maintained that it exists purely for the betterment of boys and is indifferent to all things military. But, c'mon—the uniforms, open campfires, and Buck knives? What boy would settle for *playing* army when he could almost *live* army?

Perhaps owing to the effectiveness of the Hitler Youth during WWII, or to Scouting's growing utility as an ROTC starter kit, JLCT was the closest the organization ever came to a flat-out military-style boot camp. Upon arriving there, I quickly realized the other boys were fifteen to seventeen years old. That wasn't a complete surprise, although at twelve years of age, I was so young that there was some question as to whether or not I was actually eligible for the program. After realizing there wasn't much else they could do with me, it was determined that I could stay, but then a bigger surprise came. Rather than getting instruction from nurturing father figures, we got orders at JLCT from impatient young men who came off as wannabe drill sergeants. There was already a lot about JLCT that worried me, but the worst surprise was yet to come. My tent-mate was the consensus' pick for the creepiest guy in camp. He kept me awake each night playing with cans of Sterno fuel and freely admitted that he hoped to be an arsonist when he grew up.

I was glad my troop-mates couldn't see how unhappy I was and glad they didn't know I would rather fly face-first into another cactus than endure another day in this mean and miserable camp. Although I knew they couldn't or wouldn't do anything about it, I wrote my parents, begging them to get me out of there. But by the time they received my letter, I had begun to adjust to things. And I had adjusted further still by the time Mom responded by sending me an assortment of her unbelievably delicious chocolate chip and peanut butter cookies.

The passing out of mail was another thing the camp did military style, and I eagerly opened the box without anticipating the hopeful expressions that soon surrounded me. Had I reacted in the true spirit of the Boy Scouts, I would have offered to share them. But this was war, damn it; they'd made that clear enough. So instead I closed the box and tucked it under my left arm. I then patted the handle of the Buck knife on my right hip as if to say, "Anyone touches these—I gut em." I felt bad almost immediately, not sure if the others knew my intimidating glare was intended primarily for my butthead of a tent-mate, but I saw the young drill sergeants smile at one another. It was as though they were thinking their youngest, greenest recruit was going to make it after all.

That suspicion was largely confirmed when Mr. Jamison and our troop arrived for our own wonderfully normal week at Camp Geronimo. He pulled me aside for the only real conversation I ever had with him. He told me that while they felt I was several years too young to participate in JLCT, I represented myself well and demonstrated good leadership potential. That sounded like a C+ to me, a grade completely within my comfort zone.

While not embarrassing ourselves at Camp Geronimo proved a challenge given our void in adult leadership, it was reasonably easy compared to the week I just went through. Plus, some really good things happened, like getting over my hatred of Charlie Trapp.

Charlie had joined the troop a few weeks earlier and, in small doses, struck me as a cocky little turd who desperately needed to be put in his place. But perhaps because I sensed that I needed to set a proper example, I decided to simply give him a wide berth. That strategy completely unraveled when I learned that he and I were the only ones from our troop who signed up at the stables for our horsemanship merit badge training. I didn't want another bad time, like with Shane Marks, the nudist Scout, or my pyromaniac tent-mate of last week, but there didn't seem to be any way to avoid spending time with Charlie.

That's when Charlie taught me that first impressions don't always count for much. Taken in context, I found that what I perceived as cockiness was far more self-effacing, smarter, and funnier than I had ever realized. But, to the extent that he did harbor a more endearing form of cockiness, he had the giblets to back it up. He was one of the smallest kids in the program, but he somehow drew the most spirited horse. Any time the trail opened up enough for us to allow some distance between our rides, Charlie's steed began to buck. Not only did he not panic, he stuck his left arm in the air and yelled, "Yahoooooo!" By the time we completed our badge requirements, my impression of Charlie had gone from "little fart" to "big favorite." Having Charlie as an ally rather than an adversary proved helpful even sooner than I imagined.

Just as it was at home, Mr. Jamison remained the absentee Scoutmaster who kept to himself in his tent. This left us to prepare the meal boxes arranged for us at the camp provisions center completely by ourselves. We learned quickly, however, and most of the meals we managed turned out well enough. Only when we were done prepping did Mr. Jamison emerge from his tent to eat. This pattern continued without any problems until the afternoon we were given the ingredients to make spaghetti: dry pasta, tomato paste, and ground beef. What we didn't know at the time was that they had shorted us on that evening's dinner fixings, and it didn't help that I knew nothing about preparing pasta. I over-cooked it in less water than I should have, and I didn't know I was supposed to drain it. I think I did okay browning the ground beef, but I didn't know how to deal with the extra grease that welled up in the frying pan while it cooked. In the end, I poured the greasy ground beef directly into the pan with the watery, overcooked spaghetti, topped it off with the tomato paste, and stirred.

While the meal was undeniably gross, everyone was hungry, and technically it was spaghetti, so everyone lined up for their share. I was careful to ration out small but equal amounts in everyone's bowl, and we sat down to eat. That's when I heard Mr. Jamison leave his tent and head our way for dinner. "Crap!" I said quietly. "I didn't leave anything for our Scoutmaster."

I sprang up, grabbed Charlie Trapp's bowl and dumped its meager contents in with my own. Like a waiter, I approached Mr.

Jamison as he took his seat and said, "Dinner is served." He couldn't have liked it, but he didn't complain, as that would have required him to actually say something.

Only then did I look over at Charlie and see that, like a good solider, he sat there calmly and never complained. I then assigned that night's kitchen detail and ordered Charlie to come with me. We quietly made our way to my tent where we made up for sacrificing our share of the ill-fated pasta by polishing off what remained of my mom's wonderful cookies.

Our week at Camp Geronimo concluded with a challenge that would again bring the tender age of the Scouts of Troop 39 into focus. Ozzie Denning and I were selected to compete for the Order of the Arrow. Prior to the week-long JLCT, the twenty-four hour Order of the Arrow was the toughest ordeal the Boy Scouts had to offer.

Along with our gear, Ozzie and I were plucked from camp early one morning and taken deep into the forest. The kids already gathered there were, as expected, several years our senior. The day included genuinely hard work—felling trees, removing their bark, digging trenches, and other taxing stuff. This was all to be done in absolute silence; only the program leaders were allowed to speak. What they had to say wasn't very nice, but after my week in JLCT, I was unfazed. As for Ozzie, he was always unfazed, and that made him a great guy to have along for this challenge. As you've probably deduced by now, food was hardly the highlight of Boy Scout camp, but while laboring toward your Order of the Arrow honors, they made sure that what you got to eat was particularly bad and unusually skimpy. Even so, the worst aspect of the program didn't occur until that evening.

By the time darkness fell, we were hungry and truly exhausted. That's when they ordered us to line up single file with only our sleeping bags. They then marched us deeper into the forest. Since only our leaders had flashlights, we kids stumbled and fell often while walking in the dark over an uneven forest floor. That seemed perfectly okay to the bosses with the flashlights. As we walked, a leader approached the boy at the very back of the line and, in complete darkness, whispered, "Come with me." This repeated until that leader hauled us all off one by one. Once he separated you from the group, the leader then gripped you firmly by the arm and led you well away from the still-moving line of boys. When you could no longer hear them stomping and stumbling along, he pushed you to the ground and said, "Sleep here." Then he was gone, just like that.

Dead tired and sitting alone in the cool blackness of night, there really wasn't much to do except crawl into your bedroll, pull it over your head, and call it a day. If a hungry bear happened along, your only wish was that it didn't wake you before making you its dinner.

The next morning we were awakened by the sound of a program leader marching through the area, banging a wood spoon on a metal pot, and yelling for us to wake up. Forgetting my oath of silence for the moment, I said to myself, "The sun is shining, the birds are singing, and the a-holes have returned."

Standing up, I tempted fate further by actually laughing out loud. When I collapsed on the forest floor the night prior, I had the clear impression that I was utterly alone. In the morning light, however, I could see bleary-eyed kids like me just forty yards away in every direction.

The Order of the Arrow ordeal concluded with a ceremony that relied heavily on Native American motif. The dramatic use of fire, totem poles, and drums prompted whispered wise-cracks from the ever-irreverent Ozzie Denning. I must admit, though, everyone thought the white sash they awarded us with the big, embroidered red arrow across the front was pretty cool.

All in all, my time away from home finally convinced me of what everyone else in our group already assumed—I was the undisputed senior patrol leader of Mercury Boy Scout Troop 39.

A few weeks later, with summer winding down, I celebrated my thirteenth birthday. Every boy turning that age is thrilled at the prospect of finally becoming a real, honest-to-goodness teenager. Another reason it was an extremely happy birthday for me, particularly on the heels of my JLCT experience, was the feeling that my age was beginning to catch up with my Boy Scout responsibilities.

With school back in session and the nights cooling off considerably, our attention turned from camping to regular Scout meetings. With two new recruits in the troop, the more senior of us kids busied ourselves with getting them up to the minimal rank of

Tenderfoot. That was easy in the case of Charlie Trapp, but it was a fascinating challenge in the case of Conrad Givens.

Even though Troop 39's approach to Scouting was about as casual as you could get, it was still the most structured aspect of Conrad Given's life. With his only brother being nine years his senior, he may as well have been an only child. Clearly the result of an unexpected pregnancy, his parents were much older and less involved than anyone else's. His dad had his own business building feed trailers that were in great demand by ranchers across the Southwest, and that left him largely unavailable to Conrad. His eccentric mother had no such excuse; she simply preferred to spend her time looting Native American burial grounds of valuable artifacts. And while that older brother wasn't around much either, his notoriety as a professional football player at least afforded Conrad a little something to brag about.

Conrad was small for his age with barn door ears and buck teeth that protruded out so far that he had to contort his face in order for his lips to stretch over them. This, of course, made him an easy target. Fortunately, he lived next door to my cousin Joey, who served as a surrogate sibling to Conrad and never teased him. Those who did almost always regretted it.

Conrad's initial reaction to teasing usually included tears welling up in his bespectacled eyes, but then it evaporated those tears and turned into the uncontrollable rage that boiled inside him. First, he went at his tormentors with his fists. If that didn't sufficiently vent his anger, he happily accentuated his attack with rocks, Coke bottles, or pieces of scrap iron.

His modest stature disguised impressive strength and inexhaustible energy. So the trick with Conrad was keeping that energy focused on something positive. That was easy enough in our regular meetings since being indoors limited the weaponry for his attacks. In the Scout room, Conrad was happy to follow the lead of others. On camp outs, however, it was a completely different story, and with the spring weather warming things up nicely, our next desert adventure was fast approaching.

A few weeks later, we rolled along the winding dirt roads en route to the foothills of the Luna Mountain range. While Mr. Jamison had a set of keys to the school's Scout room, he was not a school employee, and therefore he didn't have access to its vintage

Power Wagon troop carrier. That was okay, however, because he didn't really need it. As a smallish man, I expected him to drive a pint-sized import, but little about Mr. Jamison was as expected. Instead he tooled about in a huge, mid-sixties three-quarter ton crew cab pickup truck. The boxy, blue, long wheel-based Dodge featured a massive white camper with a sleeping bay that extended out over the cab of the truck. This rig was more than enough to get six Scouts to their destination.

Standard-issue Boy Scout uniforms of that era never anticipated the triple-digit heat typical of Arizona in late June. We compensated by leaving our shirttails untucked, sleeves rolled up, and neckerchiefs loosened. When Charlie Trapp removed his neckerchief altogether and tied it around his head, buccaneer style, Mercury Troop 39's signature look was born. Conrad attempted to do him one better by hacking the sleeves off his shirt, which in effect, created a Boy Scout vest. Several other boys got pretty excited about that modification, as well. They thought better of it when I reminded them that, unlike Conrad, they had mothers who actually did their laundry and would take a dim view of a mutilated Scout shirt, hand-me-down, or otherwise.

Ozzie agreed to oversee setting up the three tents we needed while I worked on the campfire pit. In short order, however, the brilliance of Conrad Givens made Ozzie a student rather than a teacher.

Foremost among Conrad's unique skill sets was his ability to dig. Massive front teeth were not the only thing he had in common with a gopher. Conrad could tunnel like no one we had ever seen. In the large dirt lot behind his father's machine shop, Conrad carved a network of tunnels so complex that even veteran Vietcong tunnel masters could get lost in it. Armed with only a small, collapsible camp shovel, he introduced us to a form of shelter that was simply the coolest—literally and figuratively.

Conrad excavated a fox hole that was roughly the dimensions of his tent, but with crisp right angles at the corners and where the walls met the floor. This was no simple dugout, and it felt like a little room. Driving his tent poles into this sunken living area allowed him to stake his tent over the subterranean hide-away at a much lower angle that the usual forty-five degrees. That lower roof angle allowed for his final brilliant touch when he covered the whole thing with the wispy branches of a just-slaughtered Greasewood bush. For Conrad, the purpose of the Greasewood branches was camouflage, but it shaded an area that was already cooler by virtue of being partially underground. Intentional or otherwise, he had created passive solar Boy Scout digs.

The afternoon proved to be good fun. While there was no dry river bed at our disposal, it was pretty desert landscape with lots of rocky hills for climbing. From the top of one of those hills, we were surprised to learn that we were not alone—there was another camp in the distance. It featured at least a dozen tents, assorted trucks and trailers, and a flag pole featuring Old Glory and another flag we couldn't quite make out. From where we were, the camp's inhabitants looked like ants scurrying about. We stayed low, like a small tribe of Indians watching a wagon train encroach on its territory. I looked back in the direction of our camp. No one was in it, and our sunken, camouflaged tents were invisible unless you knew exactly where to look. It made Mr. Jamison's faded blue behemoth look like some ancient ark abandoned in the desert.

As twilight approached, I removed ingredients from two aluminum ice chests and began preparing dinner. I asked Robbie if his dad was likely to join us. He looked at the camper that his father had been holed up in since we unloaded our gear earlier that day. Robbie shrugged and said, "I don't know why he would. He has everything he needs in that rig."

"Too bad," I thought. After the pasta fiasco at Camp Geronimo I had Mom show me the proper way to drain the ground beef and pasta before combining them with the canned spaghetti sauce. Everyone was duly impressed and eager to dig in except Conrad who arrived a little late for dinner.

He had made himself scarce since we returned from our earlier exploration of the surrounding foothills. As we cradled bowls of spaghetti in our laps, he walked up with an armload of what appeared to be walking sticks carved from the ribs of a decaying saguaro cactus. As he laid them out neatly by the fire, however, it was clear that he had whittled one end of each rib to a sharp point.

He waited until our buzzing stopped and he had our undivided attention. "Spears," he said. "There's one for each of us." Then, pointing in the general direction of the bigger camp installed in the distance beyond the hill, he continued, "We attack at midnight!"

We all laughed and Conrad was pleased. On one hand, he wanted to get a laugh, but on the other, we all knew that he wasn't exactly kidding. Conrad persisted with this plan until someone told him it was time to stop; increasingly, that job fell to me. No point in killing the fun right away, however, as midnight was a few hours away. That gave us time to sit around the campfire and tell stories while Conrad continued preparations for the attack by dipping the tips of his hand-crafted weapons in kerosene. Why strike terror into the hearts of your enemy with mere spears when they could just as easily be flaming spears?

Suddenly our fun was interrupted by the sound of boots crunching over the desert floor. We looked in the direction of the noise and saw two or three dark, silhouetted figures coming our way. The biggest of them wore what we called a Smokey the Bear hat, commonly worn by the Arizona Highway Patrol. What would those guys be doing out here? As they drew closer and their distinctive red neckerchiefs came into focus, it was clear that the guy in front was an adult. He was flanked by two boys older than any of us.

As I rose to greet them, Conrad snatched up a spear and pointed the business end in their direction. I hissed at him to cool it and he placed the butt of it on the ground and tried to look a bit more nonchalant. I was taken aback when the adult snapped a Boy Scout salute in my direction, but I managed to return the greeting in short order.

Wow. These guys were buttoned down, looking like something right out of the *Boy Scout Handbook*. We all looked disheveled and still sported our buccaneer headwear. Only Conrad and I were standing, and he was still covered in dirt from his extraordinarily productive day. The flickering campfire caused light to dance across the little, boney chest exposed beneath his one-of-a-kind Boy Scout vest. The adult finally spoke, "I am Scoutmaster Edward Goodwin of Lightfield Troop 44."

The vast nothingness an hour west of Phoenix was so thinly populated that very little qualified as a community, let alone a well-heeled one, but Lightfield came close. Sitting between Deerville and the capitol city, it was near enough that upper middle class families could buy bigger-than-average home sites for their bigger-than-average homes and still commute to Phoenix for work.

"Hi," I replied. "Welcome to our camp. We're Troop 39 from Mercury." Since he had been looking around the whole time, I thought he couldn't spot our cool tents. I was eager to show them off and planned to give Conrad the credit he was due.

But he wasn't interested in our tents. He turned to me and asked tersely, "Where is your Scoutmaster?" Given the tone of his question, I sensed it was born more of condescension than concern. I'm not sure if I wanted to protect Mr. Jamison from being embarrassed by us or to protect us from being embarrassed by him, but either way I began a campaign of what might be politely referred to as misinformation, and to my thinking, these uninvited guests didn't deserve any better. Nothing but spit-and-polish pansies, they had intruded on a camp of hard-core, guerilla Scouts without the sense to display a white flag. They were lucky I hadn't turned Conrad and the boys loose on them.

"He's not here." I answered.

"Not here!" snapped Mr. Goodwin impatiently.

"I'm sorry," I continued. "Of course he's here. I just meant to say he isn't in camp at the moment."

Goodwin looked around, agitated and confused, "Where on earth could he be?" he pressed further.

"Constellation study," I replied. "Several boys are on working on that merit badge."

He was glaring at me now, as if I still hadn't answered his question concerning our Scoutmaster's whereabouts.

"Well," I continued. "Scoutmaster Jamison takes constellation study *very* seriously. The light from this campfire, even those lights twinkling in the valley below, degrade our view of the night sky. He says it's well worth the extra effort to get as far from light pollution as possible."

Now Mr. Goodwin's expression seemed to reflect more confusion than agitation, which was exactly what I was going for, so I continued, "Anyway, he took the boys over that ridge." I pointed to a craggy, foreboding, silhouette of mountainside hundreds of yards in the distance.

"Oh…" was all Mr. Goodwin could muster.

"I don't think he'll be more than an hour," I said. "You're welcome to wait. We were just about to make some hot chocolate." That last part was true. My mom always filled a plastic container with powdered milk and dry cocoa mix. We liked to scoop two teaspoons into our enamel mugs, stir in hot water, and pretend it was coffee.

"Well...uh...no," he at last replied. Then, puffing up his chest again, he added, "Just tell him Scoutmaster Goodwin stopped by."

"Of Troop 44 in Lightfield," I interrupted.

"Yes," he added, "of Lightfield." He studied me for another moment, unsure if I was simply being thorough or just plain sarcastic. Then he and his minions turned on their heels and headed back the way they came. As they left, the balance of our group stood up and adopted defiant poses suggesting they didn't appreciate Mr. Goodwin's attitude any more than I did.

Doing a surprisingly good impression of Wally Cleaver, Ozzie Denning then said "Nice goin', Eddy." The camp again erupted in laughter. In the distance, Mr. Goodwin seemed to pause for a moment, but then continued walking. I suspect he had just decided I was being sarcastic.

That night I wondered about Mr. Goodwin and how quickly I went from hoping to impress him to starting to detest him. Was it really so wrong for him to wonder what we were doing out in the desert seemingly all by ourselves? Was it wrong that he and his charges looked like real Scouts? If Mr. Knowles were still our Scoutmaster, we would have been just as buttoned-down as Troop 44 and proud of it. I am sure we would have graciously welcomed representatives of another troop into our camp. Instead I reacted to the reality of our situation, spinning a diversionary tale while Mr. Jamison did whatever it was he did in his big, blue camper. Perhaps, when you got right down to it, I was just a little jealous. Fortunately for me, moments of self-reflection are mercifully short when you're thirteen years old.

A ROLLING STONE GATHERS NO MOSS, NOR DODGE TRUCKS FOR THAT MATTER

With school out, our regular meetings were spaced further apart since vacation plans meant too few boys were available to maintain our normal schedule. Finally, with August drawing to a close, we organized our last camp out of the summer. This one included two more new recruits, the ever-timid Peter White, and my incredibly laid back, younger brother, Jeff. While Jeff was a solid kid with an easy smile and an eagerness to help out, Peter was painfully shy. Jeff once told me that Peter hated the first day of school and any day when a substitute teacher was likely to be in class. The reason was, of course, that those were the days when attendance was most likely to be called alphabetically, last name first. Jeff said kids giggled all morning after some pretty, young substitute teacher called out for "White, Peter?"

During our meeting to discuss our last camp out, we agreed that the Luna mountain range was no good because it posed the threat of more unwanted visitors. I remembered Doug telling me about a fun trip they once had with Uncle CT to McClousky Dam, so Robbie back-channeled the suggestion to his father.

An arm of the Gila River used to meander through the scrubby, rolling landscape another hour southwest of Deerville. Its flow was seasonal, however, and made it difficult for the pioneer rancher and farmer, Clevis McClousky, to maintain his operation. His solution was to build a dam between two outcroppings of rock that bookended a narrow ravine, creating a constant reservoir of water to meet his needs. That was fifty years earlier, however, and the Gila had since been dammed up to the point where nothing reached McClousky's masterpiece any more. What little water it saw was, again, seasonal and owed itself to the contributions of small, nearby washes. That, however, was enough to ensure a low-lying oasis of lush, green vegetation that was a magnet for the area's diverse assortment of wildlife.

As we piled out of Mr. Jamison's truck, we were delighted with the fascinating variety and the silent remoteness of our location. We were now a four-tent crew and once again, Conrad took charge of setting up our shelters. We were right at the base of a large, rock-laden hill, so everything I needed for the firepit that was the nucleus of our camp was within easy reach. With that requirement quickly met, I was anxious to climb that rocky hill and get a look at our broader surroundings.

Once atop its summit, the hill rewarded me with 360-degree vistas. Everywhere you looked, the view was either interesting or beautiful or both. The nicest part was to see the horizon in every direction, and I planned to be up there for every sunrise and every sunset. Soon I was joined by some other older boys from our troop—Ozzie, Robbie, and Joey. They, too, were enthralled with the view, and for a few moments we enjoyed it together in silence.

Then, with the tents in place, the other half of the troop started its ascent up the rock-encrusted hill. Ozzie usually expressed his humor verbally, but on this occasion, he surprised us all by dislodging a large rock with his foot and kicking it downhill toward the younger boys. Since it was no larger than most of the rocks on the hill's surface, Ozzie's orb pin-balled around a bit before it stopped harmlessly, well short of the little climbers below. Inspired, Robbie heaved loose a rock bigger by half than the one Ozzie began with. While still not reaching the boys at the hill's base, Robbie's basketball-sized rock went noticeably further than the first. The boys below us howled and hooted, further encouraging our latest form of stupid recreation.

The laws of physics were evident—the bigger the rock, the farther it went. So naturally, we set about dislodging the largest ones we could manage. Ozzie and Robbie were straining against a rock far larger than our first two combined. It was a boulder, really, almost three feet in diameter. Seeing our effort to move it, the younger guys yelled out taunts, jeers, and challenges. I turned to Joey and said, "I guess this is their initiation."

Joey squinted my way and said, "It beats the heck out of a belt line."

Just then I noticed a section of pipe amid the assorted litter that had accumulated atop the hill. About six feet long and three inches in diameter, it was perfect for illustrating part two of our physics lesson—leverage.

With Ozzie and Robbie still grunting on either side of the boulder, I stepped between them and wedged the pipe beneath the craggy, brown sphere. Then I pulled down on the skyward end of the pipe and felt a little give. We let out a cheer, and the boys below continued their hollering, casually making their way to the middle of the hill. Any movement from the massive rock was reason to rejoice, but as we continued to push and pry, I began to think we should opt for a smaller target. Then, to my surprise, Joey leapt onto the tall end of the pipe and assisted our effort. Joey so rarely did anything even bordering on wrong or stupid that it never occurred to me to ask him for help. His additional weight on our make-shift pry bar made the difference. As a few smaller rocks crumbled or tumbled away from beneath it, our boulder worked itself free and began rolling down the hill.

Our amusement at having unleashed this titan quickly gave way to genuine fear. The behemoth rock was clearly not going to stop rolling without the benefit of level ground—physics lesson number three. The problem was, between our cascading boulder and the bottom of the hill, there were four young kids. Jeff and Charlie flanked Conrad and they stood three abreast about halfway up the hill. The ever-cautious Peter White was the last to set foot on the hill and the first to turn and run, even before we succeeded in dislodging the boulder. My only worry for Peter was whether we would have to send out a search party to find him when this was all over. Charlie moved to his left and Jeff to his right, leaving ample room for the boulder to pass safely between them. Conrad watched and waited. The boulder's imperfect geometry caused it to slice slightly to his right, so Conrad stepped in that direction.

Each of us atop the hill quickly exhausted our entire inventory of swear words, with the name "Conrad" neatly interspersed. We all literally had a hand in whatever was about to happen. Even if Conrad were to lie down in the boulder's path, we were responsible. He wouldn't do that, of course. We all knew what he was up to. He was attempting to position himself so the boulder merely came close to hitting him. With the boulder's relatively slow rolling speed, Conrad could easily side step it if he was on level ground. The problem was, of course, that he was facing up a steep incline so heavily layered in rocks that a mountain goat would approach it with caution.

I had gone from disparaging generations of the Givens' ancestry to simply repeating, "Don't slip...do not slip." If he did, the best Conrad could hope for was serious bodily injury, with death being the more likely outcome.

About five hundred pounds of slow-tumbling terror continued to veer slightly to Conrad's right, and he took baby steps in that direction to ensure the maximum dramatic effect. Then, at the last moment, he made two clumsy jumps to his left just as the boulder lumbered past him. The need to steady himself with his hands prevented him from completing the matador wave he clearly intended, but he did manage to yell out, "Olé!"

Never before has a sigh of relief so quickly gotten stuck in my throat, because in the next moment I realized our worries were far from over. On the level ground at the foot of the hill, directly in the boulder's path, sat Mr. Jamison's big, blue Dodge pickup, with him doing whatever it was he did inside of it.

Joey, Ozzie, and Robbie all saw it, too, and the swearing resumed, but in a hushed, almost reverent whisper, "Oh shit…Oh God…Oh crap…"

More than halfway down the hill, the boulder continued to slice to our left. At its current trajectory, I figured it would smash Mr. Jamison's truck right behind the driver's side front wheel. Even though it seemed to happen in slow motion, there wasn't time to look at the other boys or say anything. Our eyes were all locked on the horror unfolding before us.

As the boulder closed the distance between itself and the Dodge, we noticed another focal point. Where our camp leveled out was a small but handsome outcropping of rock. It was just a couple of feet high and pointed at a forty-five degree angle away from the path of the rolling boulder. Most importantly, its position, which was about eight feet away from the truck's front wheel, made it increasingly likely to influence the boulder's point of contact. If the boulder hit the outcrop on the right side, it would probably slam directly into Mr. Jamison's driver's side door. If it hit the outcrop's left side, it might only skirt the front bumper.

As the tension mounted, I thought of the hushed but distinctive tones of the sports broadcaster, Chris Schenkel, announcing ABC's Pro Bowler's Tour. I could see slow-motion images of a spinning bowling ball hooking to catch a headpin to the right or left and how the ball's path was influenced accordingly.

The boulder was definitely going to smack the rock outcrop. It crunched onto to it almost dead center, actually rolling up it a bit before the same dynamics that caused the boulder to slice left as it careened down the hill also caused it to fall off to the left side of the outcrop. The nearly square impact reduced its speed considerably, and the boulder rolled slowly to a stop just two feet directly in front of Mr. Jamison's bumper.

Robbie and Ozzie hurried down the hill to join the younger boys in examining our trophy. I stayed atop the hill, sat next to Joey, and appreciated how lucky we were. I started to think about the possible consequences of a different outcome, but it was just too hideous to consider, so I thought of something else. I thought about how weird it was to have fun acting like a kid in one moment only to realize that I was supposed to act like an adult in the next. Uncle CT had this problem all the time and was thirty years older than us. I think that was the hardest thing about Joey's childhood. As long as CT initiated the stupidity, everyone had fun. But if he caught you acting stupid on your own, he wasn't amused. As an adult, I came to know this as hypocrisy, and it was hardly unique to CT Lawton. Almost all kids expected it from all adults because of the often-used phrase, "Do as I say, not as I do." This incident was just another reminder that I wasn't ready to be an adult yet.

With the usual assortment of projects and kids' stuff to occupy the guys, the rest of the afternoon passed quietly enough for everyone except Peter White, who got more than his share of teasing. I assumed his protracted retreat from the killer boulder was the reason, but I was working on dinner by then and knew our communal food-fest would afford him some peace.

Everyone had brought a can of the beloved Dinty Moore Beef Stew for this camp out. This was a rare indulgence on the part of mothers who could cook up the real deal more economically. Cans traveled well, however, and soon we were wiping our bowls clean with slices from a misshapen loaf of squishy white bread. We washed it down with Tang, a Boy Scout favorite, and if you believed the television commercials, an astronaut favorite, too. All that was left was dessert and I sent my little brother Jeff to get the chocolate chip cookies our mom had baked for the occasion. While we waited, someone started in on Peter again, making a crack about the "boogey man in the brush."

"What's that all about?" I asked.

Four boys started talking over each other at once and poor Peter looked deflated, fearing that even I was going to start in on him. I said, "C'mon you guys—shut up! I want to hear what happened to Peter."

"Well," Peter began, "I ran down the hill away from the boulder and kept going down that little slope that leads to the bushy area by the ravine."

As he spoke, I was struck with what a nice addition Peter was to the troop. While cautious to the point of being a little jumpy, he was no dummy, particularly when it came to the desert. Unlike most of us whose houses were surrounded by crops that put the raw desert a few miles away, the Whites lived in Little Star Valley. That put them south of the Gila River, beyond the reach of the Roosevelt Irrigation District, and squarely in unaltered desert. Where Peter lived, scorpions, rattle snakes, and coyotes weren't something you went looking for—they came to you. Perhaps the other boys were considering this as well, because as we sat there with only the light of the campfire flickering across our faces, Peter's retelling of his ordeal took on the quality of a ghost story.

Peter continued, "So as I stood there, looking back up the hill, something started to growl at me. Kind of like an angry animal, but kind of different, too. When I turned to see what it was, the bushes started to shake like crazy! But wild animals don't usually act like that, ya know? They either stay very still, or they charge you, or they run away."

It stayed quiet for a second, until Charlie Trapp spoke up. "I went with Peter back to that spot in the bushes. It looked like something might have been moving around in there."

"What did you see?" I asked. "Animal tracks? Foot prints?" Everyone looked a little spooked now, and suddenly we heard a pronounced "THUD!" A rock landed in our firepit, causing a couple of its well-roasted logs to collapse into coals and send a little explosion of tiny orange sparks spiraling into the sky.

Most of the boys hollered and scrambled away toward our tent area. Poor Peter sat there frozen in fear. I was scared, too, but I stood up so that I could look around and listen. It was hard to know the direction from which the rock had come, but I guessed it came from the bushy darkness behind Peter, just beyond the light of our campfire.

Then, another small rock bounced off one of the bigger rocks that rimmed our firepit. Peter yelped and the clamoring of our returning boys made it almost impossible to separate the sounds, but I thought I heard muffled laughter coming from the area I'd been trying to see. I took two steps in that direction, and that was the only clue the charging buccaneers of Troop 39 needed.

The blur that raced by terrified as much as it impressed. They featured flashlights, hatchets, and knives and raced to their own soundtrack of warrior screams. Spheres of yellow light jerked radically about a wall of bushes and tall grass just before the boys went crashing through it. I nearly knocked Peter over in pursuit. By the time I reached them, our guys were fanned out in a semi-circle to better surround the two horrified protagonists pressed up against a steep rock wall. Our guys held their assorted weaponry menacingly in front of them.

I recognized the two boys as the Williams brothers. "Guys!" I shouted, "It's okay! I know these boys!" With their bodies clinched in the grip of adrenalin and pheromones, they eased out of their attack postures and slowly turned my way. All, that is, except Conrad. He was still completely locked in, which was horribly apparent to me and the other boys, and especially the two unfortunate pranksters quivering before him. My fear was that Conrad would project all the angst he harbored against past bullies toward the Williams brothers.

"Conrad," I continued, now using a tone that was calm, but direct. "It's okay, Conrad. These are the Williams brothers. They went to Desert Rose Elementary. I ran track against them."

We all watched carefully until Conrad's white-knuckled grip loosened slightly from his trademark saguaro rib spear. "That's okay, Greg," Conrad finally said, "That's no reason we can't enjoy a little Desert-Rose-Wise-Guy-Kid-Kabob."

Even though we were all still tense from near panic, I forced a laugh. Then the other boys joined in until finally even the Williams brothers managed weak smiles. Once they sensed that it was okay to move, they crept cautiously my way to pat me on the back and vigorously shake my hand. "It is really good to see you again," the older one said, although it seemed like he really didn't remember me.

We regrouped around the firepit, making room for the Williams brothers, and we all shared my mom's chocolate chip cookies. They explained that they lived about a mile away and had come to the dam with their slingshots. They were surprised to find us here because no one ever came out this far, except for during dove hunting season, but during that time the Williams brothers had the good sense to stay inside.

At first they were content to simply watch us, enjoying the boulder hijinks, but when Peter practically fell into their lap, they couldn't resist having some fun with him. They went home for an early dinner, but since nothing was on TV but summer reruns, they decided to come back. Again they expected to just watch us, but hearing our talk about the scare they put into Peter proved irresistible once more.

Everyone agreed that cookies around the campfire beat hacking two desert brats to death. And while we could smile about it afterwards, we all understood just how close that had come to happening.

That night I thought further about the silliness of our situation. The Williams brothers admitted that they thought we were out here alone, assuming Ozzie, by virtue of his height, was old enough to drive. They were surprised when Robbie told them his dad was in his camper the whole time. I doubt this particular drama would have played out if an adult had been in evidence.

Sure, I was responsible for the near-disaster with the boulder, and while I couldn't have done anything to prevent the near-slaughter of the Williams brothers, in a way, I would have been accountable for that, too. Enabling, another word I would not use until becoming an adult, is what I was most guilty of. By stepping in for adults who either wouldn't or couldn't step up, I made it possible for a troop to exist with what amounted to a Scout *chauffer*—since Mr. Jamison certainly wasn't a typical Scout*master*. And, as our last two outings had suggested, typical Scoutmasters can come in handy at times.

In a week I would turn fourteen, and the week after that I would start my freshman year at Deerville Union High School. I decided that was the time to retire my sweat-stained uniform. Ozzie arrived at the same conclusion, and most importantly, so did Robbie Jamison. That meant Mercury Boy Scout Troop 39 was without a Scoutmaster once more.

Then a good thing happened. Charlie Trapp's dad volunteered to be the new Scoutmaster. Maybe my quitting actually brought about a positive change? Maybe, I considered, I should think about staying in?

I might have if the Boy Scouts had offered merit badges for my new interest areas of cars, girls, and beer, but since they didn't, it was time for me to move on.

THE TOOTHLESS WONDERS

My dad didn't usually return from work bearing good news unique to me, but that's exactly what he did on a warm afternoon in late May. That day, on his way home, he had stopped at the Tamarack Tavern for a cold beer and got into a conversation with veteran farmer, rancher, and dairyman, Hollis Shales. Before it was over, they determined that I'd be just right for a summer job at Shales Ranch. I could hardly wait the four days remaining until school let out.

As a result of their chat, I began my fourteenth summer sitting atop an antiquated Farmall tractor, negotiating the patchwork of cotton and alfalfa fields that lay just south of the Roosevelt Irrigation District's canal system. Like the point on an oversized Etch-A-Sketch, I traced a series of long, straight lines and right angles, leaving a strip of scorched earth in my wake. I began my duties for Shales Ranch as a ditch burner, an occupation long since outlawed by the Environmental Protection Agency.

In the desert, it is said that if you can spit, you can become a farmer. That's because something will sprout on contact with water—this is an exaggeration perhaps, but it's largely true of irrigation ditches. Greenery sprang from cracks in their concrete and bunched up in thickets along their banks. This unwanted jungle slowed the flow of the water that otherwise fueled agri-business and kept local farmers fat and happy. I waged a summer-long battle to keep those ditches clear, and my weapon of choice was fire.

Each morning at sunrise I topped off a trailer-mounted tank with propane and puttered off to whatever section of land Hollis Shales deemed a priority. Old Man Shales drove by every couple of days to check my progress, but otherwise, I worked unsupervised. I was very happy with my job. I wasn't old enough to legally drive a car, but I had a tractor and a flame thrower and permission to use them both.

Propane fed from the pressurized tank down a long rubber hose to a five-foot length of pipe. Two pilot burners flamed gently at one end of the pipe, while a lever adorned the other end. When I squeezed the lever, I activated the flow of gas and caused an eight-foot arch of fire to roar from the burners.

Standard ditch-burning strategy involved making an initial pass at a ditch to scorch the green growth on its banks. That stage of ditch-burning was rather uneventful. The thrill came a few days later when the weeds, now dead and drying, got hit for a second time and exploded into great balls of flaming fun. Amidst the crackling flames and swirling bellows of smoke, it was good to remember two more bits of ditch-burning wisdom: keep your tractor upwind and try not to catch yourself on fire. I was usually light on details when I told Mom and Dad about my dream job.

Common sense dictated protecting oneself from the summer sun long before anyone assigned SPF factors to sunscreen. I wore a broad-brimmed hat, dark glasses, a long sleeve shirt, leather gloves, boots, and jeans. When I pulled a wet bandanna up across the bridge of my nose to filter the smoke, I perfected a look that would turn any girl's head, provided she was into Sandinista guerrillas. While this stylish ensemble prevented the sun and fire from turning my skin into a leathery beef jerky, it didn't do much to help with the problem of weight loss.

If you want to slim your waistline, forget about the latest fad diets—try standing within hair-singeing distance of open flames in triple-digit summer heat instead. It doesn't matter what you eat or how much you drink, the pounds just melt away. I was already on the skinny side when I began my torch-wielding reign of terror. By the time it ended, the Boy God of Fire was another fifteen pounds lighter. I looked like a heroin chic fashion model.

Fortunately for my health, I didn't get to spend the whole summer burning ditches. I forgot the first rule of summer employment: make sure to pace yourself so the job actually lasts all summer. I got so caught up in the apocalyptic appeal of my work that I finished several weeks ahead of schedule. Old Man

Shales mistakenly assumed I was a go-getter and, rather than sending me home early, he generously set about finding me other assignments.

It was easy to take Hollis Shales for granted as a gentleman farmer. The old man was perpetually leaning over the wheel of his truck, peering at the work his minions needed to get done while his grown, stout adult sons spent an inordinate amount of time parked in front of Clyde's, a rundown little combination pool hall and poker parlor. But I was happy to see them for the talented cowboys they really were, especially when they rode in behind their big herd of young bulls for processing day at the center of the farm's large, open stock pens.

Once inside the corral, my job was to hoop and holler and herd the ornery young bovines through a series of long, narrow wooden chutes that finally led to a big, pipe-welded, V-shaped branding chute. I shooed in the bellowing, wild-eyed bulls nose to tail, and tried in vain to keep the big, gooey mounds they left in their wake off my quickly greening, (formerly black) high-top basketball shoes.

As I scrambled about the pen, I romanticized the experience as my own version of "running with the bulls." But coming of age for the quickly maturing cattle is what the exercise was really all about. Once they got squeezed into that branding chute, I realized I was part of something more akin to "the ruining of the bulls."

Each young bull was set upon by a trio of cowboys with the speed and efficiency of an Indy car pit crew. One cowboy at the bull's head clipped a metal tag into its right ear before taking what looked tree branch cutters to chop off the proud young bull's horns. For the next five seconds or so, a fine stream of blood squirted from the center of the newly knobby bumps. A cowboy on the bull's left rear flank stabbed the bull's hip with a huge hypodermic needle of meds while the ranch hand directly opposite him seared the Shales Ranch SR brand into the smoldering right hide. Finally, the same cowboy who administered the meds grabbed a big hook-shaped knife, reached down between the bull's legs, and performed the *pièce de résistance*—he lopped off the bull's testicles and tossed them into big tubs of cool water. As quickly as they filed in, the freshly minted steers were ejected from the cruel machine and left to stroll about dazed and confused, pondering the painful ordeal that just befell them. The exercise was intended to make them easier to fatten up for the beef market, but I decided then and there that if I ever had a son, I would spare him the meaningless ritual of circumcision.

The water tubs that their wobblies were so unceremoniously splashed into were there to keep the delicacies fresh for the Rocky Mountain oyster feast that would follow. People always say they taste like chicken, but they don't. They taste more like, well…bull balls.

With that day of work behind us, Old Man Shales came though yet again, and my last assignment just might have been the best. In the first light of the next morning, I found my emaciated butt riding the fender of the biggest, newest, John Deere tractor in the Shales fleet. At the controls was Reed Tandy, the older brother of my sarcastic friend, Jim. A slight family resemblance was the only clue that the two were siblings. The younger Tandy towered over his so-called big brother, and while Jim was as boisterous as he was big, Reed was soft-spoken with a sense of humor dryer than the desert breeze. We had more than his kid brother in common. In September, we would both return to school—only Reed would be teaching classes while I conspired to ditch them. In the meantime, we prepared to chop ninety acres of corn into cattle feed. My job was to operate the cutter's chute and direct the fresh-cut silage into the waiting beds of the grain trucks that drove slowly alongside us.

I was fascinated with the trio of well-worn, owner-operated grain trucks. The two-ton Chevys had rounded features common to trucks of the mid-1950s, and even those areas that were supposed to sport right angles did not. The wooden sideboards of the grain beds either bowed out or curved in as much as twenty degrees. Copious amounts of tattered rope and twisted bailing wire kept them from listing even further. Multiple coats of oxidized paint faded in and out of one another, accented by patches of surface rust. The resulting hue could best be described as dusty pizza.

While this fleet was in sharp contrast to our sparkling new tractor, the drivers of these trucks were merely an extension of the trucks' disrepair. The sun had darkened their white skin and lightened their dark hair in equal proportion. The resulting monotone was without the compensating benefits of the hair conditioners and skin moisturizers that made that look work for tennis pros. There was no healthy contrast of tanned skin to light eyes and bright teeth. The whites of their eyes weren't all that white—glassy yellow was more accurate. Teeth—white or otherwise—were in very short supply. I don't believe you could have assembled a full set of teeth between them.

Their attire did nothing to salvage their appearance. I know what you're thinking, but many *ruralistas* did, in fact, have a keen sense of style. That season, the fashionable farm laborer was sporting snug-fitting Wranglers, sensible boots, a comfortable t-shirt and a ball cap, promoting his tire company of choice. These guys went way past simply thumbing their noses at the conventions of desert cowboy chic. Their ill-fitting mix of shiny, threadbare slacks and yellowing, long-sleeved, white shirts seemed more appropriate to a northeastern skid row than a working ranch in the southwest.

We dubbed the biggest of them Hoss, the smallest of them Little Joe, and the least descript of them Adam.

While the *Bonanza* monikers were fun, we usually just referred to the brothers en masse as the "Toothless Wonders." We assumed they were brothers. The close-set eyes and underdeveloped ears led us to believe they had been dipped out of the shallow end of a common gene pool. We had to make such assumptions about the surly trio since our efforts to communicate with them were met with a series of terse, disinterested grunts. I took this anti-social behavior as evidence that they were on the lam. I wondered aloud where Hollis Shales dug up these guys. Reed speculated that they were holdovers from the days of migrant farming, following seasonal crops from one locale to the next.

They drove within three feet of the right side of our tractor for the next two weeks while we chopped down the corn field. We crept down one end of the field and then up the next, towing the corn chopper behind us. It worked like a huge wood chipper, gathering in the corn, cutting it into bovine-bite-sized bits, and then rifling it out a chute that extended skyward like the neck and head of a brontosaurus. From my spot on the fender, I operated a control arm that aimed the flow of freshly cut feed out the chute and into the truck beds. Had I slipped from there, it's not likely that Reed could have stopped the tractor before the cutter's blades made me one with the silage. Once again, I spared my parents the mundane details of my work.

Reed and I moved easily between long stretches of silence and sophisticated conversation. In one afternoon alone, we worked out solutions for world hunger, the conflict in the Middle East, and unwanted back hair.

Sometimes it was nice to just listen, especially on those occasions when Reed shared stories from his days in high school. That's how I came to learn he was actually on hand for the legendary Watermelon Bowl, a football game that most had only heard about.

Back then, there was an old, reclusive millionaire land holder in the area who was usually off in Africa on safari, but who always had the good nature to lay in several rows of watermelon and cantaloupe in one of his most remote fields near the canal next to a tall stand of shady cottonwood trees. When the mid-afternoon heat caused the young, early-to-work labor set to call it quits, they met up at that spot. The boys lowered the melons into the canal in gunny sacks to cool them down, drank six-packs from squeaky Styrofoam ice chests, and enjoyed a good swim.

There was nothing unique in any of this, and at the time I worked for Old Man Shales, the practice was still pretty common. But on the fateful afternoon of the Watermelon Bowl, ten years earlier, the BS and bravado got to flying around pretty good between the seven participants. Several of those boys were among the best football players the area had ever produced.

It wasn't so much that they squared off in a ferocious dirt-clod meets pigskin conflict right there in the melon-lined, but otherwise freshly disked-under field; it's the other imagery from the game that stayed with me. Reed said they had intricately carved their watermelon rinds into neatly-fitting football helmets. As they played, the sticky red juice tricked down to co-mingle with the dirt from the field and the blood from their abrasions. The messy mosaics were in sharp contrast to their farmer-tanned torsos. Their once white bodies were clad only in an assortment of jockeys, boxers, and their ever-present cowboy boots. Reed's only regret was that no one had a camera on hand to capture the moment, but because I was a budding young artist, I recall thinking that I would commit the visual to canvas someday.

On the tractor, we knew our lazy conversations could be interrupted at any moment by the shrill cry of a varmint falling prey to the technology in tow. It was apparent we were not simply cutting a cornfield, but also the eco-system it supported. Several times each day we watched wild cats and rabbits dive deeper into the rows of corn hoping to avoid the mechanical fury of our advance. We became increasingly concerned about the growing menagerie within the ever-shrinking cornfield. We feared our final pass would result in a slaughter of B-movie proportions. Then there were the bugs—the kind you only encounter when you carve through a stand of seven-foot tall vegetation. We always alerted one another to the arrival of a mutant insect. "Excuse me, Reed, but a petite, glass-winged rhinoceros is preparing to eat your shoulder."

Alone in their trucks, the Toothless Wonders were oblivious to such details. They weren't drawing analogies between our diminishing cornfield and the plight of the rain forest. They had but one income-influencing focus: delivering loads of silage as quickly as possible. It was like a giant, gas-powered juggling routine. By the time one truck was half-full, another was pulling in behind it having just emptied its load. Meanwhile, the full third truck was racing to the feed lot scales at break-neck speed. That pattern went unbroken until one afternoon when we rounded the southeast corner of the field and saw a sheriff's vehicle waiting at the entrance to the property in the shade of a cottonwood tree.

Reed steered away from the field and rolled over the freshly cut stubble between us and the squad car. As we walked toward the vehicle, Deputy Sheriff Richard George, a mutual friend, emerged and yelled, "How's that new John Deere doing for ya?" That was code talk for, "I have nothing to discuss with you, but how would you like to get out of the sun for a few minutes?" The length of those conversations was in direct proportion to the heat index. The higher the temperature, the longer the conversation lasted. When Richard inquired as to the relative well-being of Reed's dog, I knew the chin wag was drawing to a close.

As we walked back toward the tractor, I noticed Team Toothless waiting at the far end of the field. It wasn't like them to leave an inefficient distance between our chopper and their trucks. But there they were. They looked like warriors, lined up three abreast, at the opposite end of a battle field. They waited conspicuously until Sheriff George had driven from sight before racing up behind us, single file. To our surprise, the one we called Hoss jumped from his truck and bounded toward us. "Wud'e wont?" barked Hoss.

Thanks to his teaching experience, Reed spoke passable moron. "What did he want?" Reed asked, confirming his understanding of the question.

"Yeah," Hoss replied, calmer now. "John Law. Wud'e wont?"

Reed listened intently then replied, "Oh, he didn't want anything. He's an old friend, just stopped by to say hello."

Hoss let out a sigh of relief so thick and tangible that Reed and I leaned back to avoid it. He then confessed through a jack-o-lantern grin, "We'uz worried. None of us gots driver's licenses."

Suddenly the Toothless Wonders seemed more vulnerable than moronic. It was an interesting confab, one that still creeps into my consciousness. Whenever I drive by a field and see a lone tractor plowing the earth, I wonder about its driver. It could be a naïve fourteen-year-old kid, someone with a master's degree in education, or a hapless fellow in need of dental work just hoping a policeman won't inquire about his nonexistent driver's license.

Our last few days together were uneventful. Our final pass didn't yield the carnage we anticipated. The animals got wise the night before and quite literally moved on to greener pastures.

We finished with the cornfield just days before school started. I said goodbye to Reed. After racing away with their final loads of feed, the Toothless Wonders didn't return to say *adios*. That's okay, since I guess a group hug was pretty unlikely anyway.

I hadn't thought much about that summer until years later when I paid a visit to one of my brothers. His young son looked up from the bicycle he was working on and ran over to greet me using grammar common to that of six-year-olds. A double negative rang in my ears as he flashed a grin that wasn't the least bit self-conscious about the two gaping holes awaiting the arrival of his permanent teeth. His cheeks and forehead were smudged with greasy dirt.

He reminded me that we all go through a Toothless Wonder phase. Some of us just stay in it longer than others.

UNEASY RIDER

Migrating from grade school to the much larger high school in Deerville was pretty big stuff for the forty of us who made up the graduating class at Mercury Elementary. We comprised the second largest contingency there. The kids feeding in from the further-flung and more isolated grade schools in the thirty-mile circle that surrounded Deerville, namely Mesquite and Hassyampa Elementary Schools, contributed only thirty and twenty new freshmen respectively. Our group was completely overwhelmed, however, by the nearly seventy kids who moved seamlessly together after already spending eight years at Deerville Elementary, just a few blocks away.

Aside from dealing with all the new challenges of a disorienting campus and confusing combination lockers, we also had to contend with an existing dominant clique, so we were always on the lookout for any familiar face.

But it wasn't all bad. Though we were lost, dorky freshman, we were at least finally in high school and I, for one, was spared the inconvenience of waiting in front of the house each morning before enduring a very long bus ride to a far-away high school. That was thanks to my older brother, Doug. He was a junior and drove me in his classic 1964 VW Bus. Sure, I was generally the target of his wickedly sarcastic wit, but I still got to ride up front with him, at least until we reached the home of his best friend, Kent Morrison. There I was relegated, quite literally, to the back of the bus and remained concealed behind its hippie flag curtains until they could safely deposit me at a remote corner of the campus. Then they could then resume cruising before class without the humiliation of being seen with an embarrassing kid brother.

High school brought other exciting changes, too. The relaxed morning band classes and a mix of after school sports made things easier for me. I was able to let go of my constant search for those familiar old faces and begin to enjoy friendly new ones.

With the learning curve of the freshman year behind me, I enjoyed that fun-filled summer working at the farming and ranching combine of Old Man Shales, and all too quickly it was time to return to Deerville High, but this time as a legitimate sophomore. In so many ways, returning to high school was much easier than first discovering it. I was more knowing, confident, and enthusiastic—and I'm sure that combination caused my parents equal parts hope and concern.

On one hand, I had known for a few years that I wanted to be a commercial artist when I grew up and was lucky enough to have some classes and teachers that allowed me to focus my energies there. The downside was that anything that didn't directly support my priorities bored me immensely, including a few must-have college prep courses.

Of greater concern was my sudden eagerness to grow up. I had taken an interest in driving, the opposite sex, and alcohol, pretty much in that order, and I didn't see the sense in waiting to experiment with them in advance of reaching any adult-imposed age requirements. There was a common argument in our home that year: I consistently reminded my mom that I was *all of* fifteen, and she consistently responded angrily, "That's right, you are *only* fifteen!" That refrain was repeated so often that it still rings in my ears today.

I know some of my focus on the new and grown-up stuff had to do with my choice of fresh Deerville-bred friends. Steven Brickhouse, for instance, was even more formidable that his name suggested. Pound for pound, he was the toughest kid I ever met, as evidenced by his four-year domination of a premium wrestling weight class. But in spite of being smart and generally easygoing, like all of us I suppose, Steven had a screw loose.

My friend, Eric Bruce, once told me that he and Steven climbed the rickety, abandoned water tower on the south side of town. Eric passed on climbing up ahead of Steven knowing he was strong enough to shake the old metal tower and laugh while Eric swayed atop helplessly. He felt much safer when Steven agreed to go up ahead of him. That is, until Eric was halfway up the tower and felt Steven peeing down on him from above. Steven never did anything that ornery to me—we mostly laughed a lot—but he could still be scary.

Two boys strolling along Deerville's dirt canal road, draining a couple of Dr. Peppers sounds pretty idyllic, right? It was, until the faster and stronger of us noticed a fountain of golden sparks shooting up from an open air welding shop. The shop was close enough that, with one hefty throw, Steven was able to send his Dr. Pepper bottle flying into it. Rather suddenly, the tranquil setting quickly devolved into the sound of smashing glass, a tirade of angry swearing, and the sight of Steven laughing and racing away.

Another new friend with influence over me, was Bobby Ceveria. Bobby was a year older than me, a junior, and a laconic charmer. He had a license but never a car, didn't work, never had money, and didn't seem to care. He simply displayed enough friendly indifference that people seemed happy enough to offer him rides and drinks, which he graciously accepted. I was only too happy to be one of his benefactors.

Fortunately, before my new friends and I were able to get into much trouble, the end of my sophomore year came along and allowed me to ease back into the comforts of summer. Once again, my dad came through for me by lining up a great summer job.

New construction was conspicuous in our rural setting, but particularly when it was on a highly visible curve on the primary road that connected Deerville to every community east of it, including Phoenix. Along that road, there used to be a well-known but little visited World War II era hut known as the Tamarack Tavern. Amos and Audrey Emmons wisely purchased the property and knocked down the old watering hole. Then they cleared away all the namesake trees that once surrounded it.

A mountain of sun-baked Mexican adobe bricks gave rise to a much anticipated new steakhouse, saloon, and dance hall called The Bull Dogger. Dad stopped in before they opened, and they told him the dishwasher job was mine if I didn't mind an awful lot of hard manual labor. He assured them I didn't, and he was right—I was thrilled to have a job waiting for me. The pay was at the bottom end of the restaurant scale, but it came with lots of hours—Tuesday through Sunday, 5p.m. until 11p.m.

The new steakhouse was about five miles from our place and I used that as excuse to buy a brutally used motorcycle from

Doug's friend, Kent. Dad had offered to let me use his heavy, metal-clad, vintage Cushman scooter, but I was only too happy to dig into the money I was saving for a car since Kent was selling an actual Harley-Davidson. Never mind that he was a natural-born mechanic able to keep the leaky little 65 cc piece of crap up and running. I, on the other hand, pushed the reluctant, under-powered motorcycle more often than I actually rode on it.

Once it opened, all were anxious to get a look at the new Bull Dogger and business was brisk. Initially, the hours proved even longer than anticipated and I found myself hunched over three steaming sinks each night until well after the kitchen had closed.

Rightly, Amos predicted that things would slow down and place fewer demands on each of us. When that happened, the job got really fun. Friday and Saturday nights kept hopping, and live music always boomed through the wall that separated my section of the kitchen from the dance hall on the other side. The other nights, however, slowed to include long, quiet spells, and both of the Emmons' were great about encouraging me to get out of the lonely kitchen. A fixture on his barstool, Amos would hand me a pocketful of house quarters marked with generous swatches of red nail polish. He wanted me to make sure the bar's juke box was always playing—and with that done, he liked the sound of brightly colored balls clicking about the pool tables. I got plenty of use out of house quarters there, as well.

Amos and Audrey presented an interesting contrast. She was the ultimate people person, charming guests in and out of the restaurant. He, on the other hand, seemed to hate everybody. It took me a while to figure out he wasn't really a racist, as he disliked everyone equally. Fortunately, they were both extremely kind to me, owing I suppose, to the hard-working contrast between me and their own absentee kids, who put precious little energy into their family's business.

Amos was as handsome as Audrey was pretty, but where he made his biggest contribution was at the massive, open-flame, mesquite grill that was the focal point of the cavernous dining room. He varied the height of the five-by-ten foot grill by spinning a giant wagon wheel connected to a series of wrought-iron gears and chains. Salivating customers looked on as steaks flew off the flames, onto a plate and landed in front of them with nary a loss of sizzle.

While all was exciting and new at The Bull Dogger, things at home were a comfortable repeat of the previous summer. Mom took the four younger kids up to the cool pines of the family cabin where they remained until school resumed after Labor Day. That was a routine I remembered well as a younger boy because my birthday fell at the end of August and was always an after-thought. With gift options limited to what could be found at the nearest hardware store, I had more flashlights and hand tools than any kid on the planet. My birthday cakes were even weirder and usually decorated with my aunt and uncle's martini condiments.

With last year's job at the Shales farm, however, I got to stay home with Doug and Dad instead of going up to the cabin with Mom—at last. The biggest change this time involved my schedule. Where we all got very early starts the year prior, I was now the odd man out, leaving for work shortly before they arrived home and still fast asleep well after they left each morning.

One constant of this odd arrangement that didn't change were Dad's protracted weekend absences. He left directly for the mountains from work on Friday afternoon and drove straight to the office really early on Monday morning. That meant Doug didn't see Dad from early Friday until late Monday, and my schedule only allowed me to say "hi" on my lone Monday night off.

You might think that arrangement would prove too tempting for two unsupervised teenagers, but it really didn't. We'd figured out the previous summer that anything beyond the smallest gathering could evolve into a bigger mess than we were interested in cleaning up, and we knew the irrigation ditch in front of our house was the very definition of an "attractive nuisance" for even a sober driver. As a result, it was much easier to have just a few friends over now and again, but even that happened rarely. Mostly, it was calm and quiet, and given that Friday and Saturday nights were, by far, the longest and hardest at the sink, that was fine with me.

And that's how summer rolled by, week in and week out, until late one Friday morning when I realized it was the beginning of August. Working at the steakhouse meant that, for two months, I had seen a lot more of my friend's parents than I had seen of my friends, so I was aching to socialize with kids my own age. I realized how long it had been since I'd attended the Friday night youth center dances.

Deerville's youth center was a remodeled former bowling alley out on the west end of town and its well-attended dances were organized and chaperoned by the local Catholic Church. As un-fun as that sounds, they featured reasonably good local and regional bands playing in subdued nightclub lighting.

Penguinesque nuns did troll the dance floor to watch for young lovers grinding a bit too earnestly during the slow songs, but they were comically oblivious to the mutual touching and spiked drinks that abounded in the darker recesses of the building's corners. And outside in the parking lot, well, that is where the real fun was and where the grown-ups seemed unaware of the "anything goes" atmosphere. It was my favorite place to hang out, even if just to have a beer, laugh, and catch up with friends.

Attending the Friday dances, however, required playing hooky from work on the second busiest night of the week. I would have put the possibility completely out of my mind if it wasn't for the unique temptation sitting idly beside the house—my uncle Robert's truck.

For the past two years, the border of our backyard had been defined by a two-bedroom, two-bath, single-wide mobile home. Shared by my Grandma Martin and the eleventh of her twelve very grown children, Uncle Robert was a thirty-something bachelor. It was unclear whether he was supposed to be taking care of her or the other way around, but either way, it was nice to have them back there. If you've always competed with more than forty first cousins for face time with your grandma, you can appreciate the fact that "possession is nine-tenths of the law."

Uncle Robert drove a long commute to labor at an evaporative cooler factory on the west side of Phoenix. I'm not sure how good the money was, but it didn't matter much because his living arrangements afforded him a large amount of disposable income. That allowed him to drive home one day in a brand new, black with gold trim Shelby Cobra convertible. It would be worth a fortune today, but it was his sole vehicle and he had no carport to park under, so he would have seriously devalued it in no time.

His overbearing older brothers pounded this point into him until he finally relented and went back to the dealership. He returned home with not one, but two replacement cars. The first was the aforementioned truck. It was a handsome off-white and yellow long bed Ford F-150. The second was the now forgotten and even then underappreciated little sports car called the Mercury Capri. A Mercury in badge only, the peppy German import was a kick to drive, and that's what Uncle Robert did every Friday morning. He'd drive the Capri to work on that day only and then spend the weekend in town with his girlfriend *du jour*. As a result, the truck just sat, un-driven, every weekend.

I was thirty days away from sixteen when I would legally be able to drive myself, but right then, I only had a learner's permit. Since having company would be nice either way, I decided it might as well be a licensed driver who could also provide a reasonable degree of safe cover. Before really thinking it through, I rang up Bobby Ceveria, and of course, he thought it was a smashing idea. That was all the encouragement I needed to phone The Bull Dogger and tell Audrey in a punky voice that maybe I wasn't 100%. She concluded it wasn't worth the risk to have me handling public utensils and besides, I suspect she was anxious to press her own kids into service for a change.

As was the custom during midday afternoons when we were the only two around, I wandered back Grandma's way for a casual visit. The heat had yet to force her in from the generously covered deck that faced into our backyard. As I joined her in its shade, I was pleased to confirm that Uncle Robert's parked truck couldn't be seen from her trailer. After a respectful visit, I excused myself as though it was time for the usual get-ready-for-work routine. My ruse took some effort because, given that this was the first exciting nonsense I'd been up to in ages, it felt a lot more exciting than it was.

A while later I was in appropriately smooth duds and driving toward town. I took the most remote way I could find to slip unnoticed into the down-market chunk of town that included the Ceveria abode. I was glad Bobby came out straight away. I went around to the passenger's side and yielded the wheel to Bobby. Looking pretty sharp himself, he slid our chariot into reverse and away we went.

Bobby, never one in a hurry, crept up Watson Avenue, one of the roads that allowed passage over the canal bridge en route to Main Street. He then surprised me by slowing to turn left onto the canal's dirt road. Then I saw why. Through the windshield, the setting sun cast a gorgeous amber glow on the willowy shapes of two cut-off clad girls strolling slowly along its bank.

They narrowed to single file on Bobby's side of the truck and stopped to allow him room to safely squeeze by. Bobby, barely even rolling, took the opportunity to apologize for any dust. Their simple acknowledgement that he hadn't created any was all the encouragement he needed to come to a complete stop. In no time, he had these lovely strangers engaged in easy conversation.

He directed most of his charm at the cute alpha blond while her equally compelling brunette cousin seemed content to hang back and simply listen as things played out. They were from Glendale, north of Phoenix, and doing their annual sleepover with a grandmother who lived just beyond a thick wall of dust-covered oleanders on my side of the road. After Bobby casually sold the harmless nature of the dance, he suggested that by joining us they could break up the monotony and take in a bit more of the local scene.

To our collective amazement, I think even to that of the brunette's, the blond said she would "be right back" and then she bolted around the front of the truck and through a little gate that cut-through the thick vegetation. Small talk continued with the clearly quieter brunette, and in remarkably short order the blond bounced backed through the thicket and announced that they would join us. "Can we have a half-hour to get ready?" the blonde asked.

"That's exactly how long our next errand will take." Bobby smiled. "See you here in thirty minutes."

As we waited at the convenience store for any acquaintance of legal drinking age who was willing to quench his thirst in exchange for making a buy for us, we contemplated our incredibly good fortune. Even unflappable Bobby admitted we had a better chance of being smacked by a meteoroid than scoring cute, out-of-town girls en route to the dance.

Motivated by the mounting momentum of my bold move to get the night off, I went big on the beer buy. Two cases of quality brew and a six-pack tip to our buyer. It wasn't all for us, of course. But since I wanted to hang in the parking lot that night and visit with as many friends as possible, I didn't want to worry about not being able to offer them a cold Coors.

Next, we backed the truck up to the ancient Deerville Ice Company. I pumped it full of change and a mountain of cubes spilled out into the bed of the truck. Again, I went overboard, filling the truck until its bed was covered. "Don't worry about it," offered Bobby. "Others are going to throw stuff in there, too. We'll fill it up."

He was right, of course. But I did, at least, break our beer haul from their two cases and into eight individual six-packs because that made for a more dramatic aesthetic presentation. Bobby smiled at my preoccupation with such visual details.

The girls were waiting at the appointed time and place as Bobby eased our contraband-laden, borrowed ride to a stop. In nicer clothes and wearing just enough make-up, they were even prettier than before. It was hardly subtle, or unnoticed, that the quietly confident brunette eased up to my door while the high-energy blonde raced around to get in on Bobby's side. Seems everyone was getting everything they could hope for that night.

With nightfall essentially upon us, I was glad Bobby had the presence of mind to finally turn on the headlights. Three seconds later, I wished he had also thought to look back before backing the truck onto the bridge at Watson Avenue. Suddenly, the screeching of the car tires on pavement had us all bracing for a crash.

Thanks goodness it never came—otherwise, Bobby's supposed meteoroid shower would have been the only way to explain a dented-up truck sitting in Uncle Robert's parking spot. I exhaled loudly and briefly contemplated the existence of a higher being. I soon realized that if there was a God, he was working in mysterious ways that evening, as there was no mistaking the familiar red and blue twirling lights that now engulfed our vehicle. Bobby had backed out directly in front of a Deerville police car.

Two humorless policemen circled the car, flashlights drawn and questions flying. As my dream night quickly imploded into a nightmare, I was at first unaware of the carload of kids who came upon us expecting to cross onto Main Street and turn west to the dance. Instead, they fixated on the scene as the police sent our attractive, mysterious dates on their way. I'm sure the girls' grandma was shocked to see them back so soon. The excited witnesses then marveled as the officers moved six-pack after six-pack from the bed of the truck to the trunk of their patrol car.

While I uncomfortably endured an interrogation at the police headquarters, I had no idea that, at the dance we never made it to, our legend grew with each dramatic retelling of the story.

As for my story, the police chief was losing patience. It really was my uncle's truck, but I couldn't prove it because he was unreachable in Phoenix. I really did have living, breathing parents, but there was no phone service up to the family cabin in the rim country. Awkward, yes, but true.

Obviously, I could have cleared up the mess with a call to Grandma Martin. She could have confirmed that I had apparently "borrowed" her son's truck, but I did not want to do that. I wanted to think I was sparing the old girl some considerable stress, but I was looking out for my own stress levels, too. Calling Grandma would confirm a disastrous conclusion to the affair, and on at least some level, I guess I hoped to keep the damage to a minimum.

I think the police chief wanted to believe me. He looked at a form on his desk and said, "Under age driver, possession of alcohol, and unauthorized use of a vehicle. I could easily use this to justify arresting you for felonious grand theft." My wide-eyed gulp was clearly audible, but I rightly guessed this was my time to sit quietly and listen. "Quite a night for a fifteen-year-old," he continued, and in that moment I could see my mom's features on his face.

Then, mercifully he said, "Here's what I'm gonna do." He stood, pulled open the top drawer of the file cabinet behind him and continued, "I have a folder up here that I go through once and awhile. If I don't see or hear from you at all between now and this time next year I'll throw this away as though none of this ever happened. If we should cross paths before then, this will be the start of an ugly rap sheet that will dog you the rest of your days. Does that sound fair to you?"

"Yes, sir," I sincerely replied. Then he surprised me yet again.

"Since there is no one to be responsible for you, I'm going to release you into the custody of the Ceveria family."

I immediately flashed on something a comedian once said about putting Orson Wells in charge of the Twinkies. He did not elaborate on how long I was to stay with them, but I wasn't going to ask either. It was simply high time to get out of there and deal with whatever came next as it happened.

Back at the Ceveria home, things were merely weird, but not unbearable. It was just a part of the experience that needed to be endured until I could make an escape, get home, and restore Uncle Robert's truck to its rightful parking spot.

The spartan interior of the Ceveria home owed more to lack of resources than to a minimalist sense of design. My impression was that there hadn't been a Ceveria man on the scene for some time, which might have explained his mother's apathy toward her middle son's predicament. Younger brother Timmy, however, was most impressed and enthusiastic, something that probably depressed Mrs. Ceveria even further. Eventually, Bobby's older brother popped in and put on a big show of yelling at us. Given that he was a pretty accomplished screw-up in his own right, I couldn't take it too seriously but I remained respectfully quiet just the same and, soon enough, he was gone.

Bobby was so accustomed to being catered to by others that he was, unsurprisingly, a lousy host. He foraged around enough to fashion a meager meal for himself and told me to help myself to whatever I scrounged up. Despite the half-hearted invitation, I wasn't really hungry and would not have depleted their clearly limited food inventory even if I was.

Strangest of all, there was never any discussion of what being released into their custody actually entailed. I guess I was the only one concerned about that. While I didn't simply want to get up and leave, I didn't like feeling that I was in their way either. I watched TV and quietly chatted with Bobby. Mrs. Ceveria exited early without bothering to tell her boys goodnight. Tim was always a sweetheart and excused himself before turning in, so I took that opportunity to tell Bobby to head to bed whenever he pleased. I said I would just relax and take my chances at getting home again at the first sign of light. And that is just what I did—I slipped out silently at around 5 a.m.

Amazingly, the first and only car I saw upon slipping out of town on a quiet back road was another Deerville patrol car. I waved casually from a hand draped across the steering wheel and the policeman reciprocated in kind. Perhaps he did not connect my profile or the truck with the chaos of last night, or if he did, he saw no point in making an issue of it now. Twenty minutes later, I eased the truck back into the spot from which I had taken it the afternoon before.

By mid-afternoon I was starting to realize how lucky I'd actually been. Sure, my risky move had ultimately met with disastrous results, but given the police chief's forgiving attitude, I emerged from the entire fiasco unscathed. As I walked across the backyard to visit with Grandma Martin, it was not just to keep up appearances, but also to get back to normal and put the whole episode behind me as quickly as possible.

What Grandma Martin did next was the verbal equivalent of cracking me in the head with her cane. She knew I'd taken Uncle Robert's truck and gotten myself into some pretty hot water in the process. She wouldn't volunteer anything else, except that she knew I had a few very long and uncomfortable days ahead of me. In spite of my confused shock, I opened a negotiation. By the time we finished talking, she agreed to let me be the one to explain myself to my parents.

Given the bomb Grandma Martin dropped on me, I entered The Bull Dogger expecting to see a look of hurt and betrayal on the faces of Amos and Audrey. It turned out, however, that their only concern was for the state of my health. Their assumption that my subdued attitude was tied to getting past yesterday's stomach bug reminded me that they were not Deerville people with all the same social connections—instead, they were from the town of Goodrich to the east. As such, the steakhouse was the closest thing I had to a sanctuary until Dad returned home in two days.

Two days, it seemed, was just enough time for my gears of self-preservation to start whirling. My afternoon meetings with Grandma Martin had been so normal and drama-free that I could not help but think about how far I could push the boundaries of my promise to her without quite breaking it. Certainly, she wasn't expecting me to greet my father with "Hi, Dad, welcome home. Boy, did I get into some deep shit while you were away." Instead, I thought she understood that I needed to pick the optimal moment.

But what if the optimal moment took a while, like maybe after the whole family reunited a month later? Why ruin everyone's summer, especially mine? Better still, wouldn't it be great if I could just wait until this time next year, when I could slap my knee and say, "That good ol' boy police chief has thrown away my pesky little file by now!"

I was in the house when Dad got home from work on Monday and was prepared to greet him as normally as possible, but I never got the chance. "I want to see you outside," he said tersely looking right past me.

"Crap!" I thought to myself. I did not believe Grandma had betrayed me, but could her source have somehow gotten to my Dad?

Dad was leaning on his old, white International pickup as I walked out to explain myself, but he held up his hand and asked me not to say anything. He'd heard about it all day at work from Joe Paddington.

That was worse than any scenario I could have imagined. Joe was an obnoxious co-worker of my dad's and a barely tolerable jerk under the best of circumstances. The problem was that Joe's own ne'er-do-well son, Benny, had come home from the dance with the epic legend of my failed escapade. Joe could not have been more pleased to realize he was the one breaking the tawdry news to my dad about his skirt-chasing, beer-drinking, truck-stealing, JAILBIRD SON!

I tried to speak again, if only to apologize, but Dad again raised a hand, signaling me to remain silent. Finally, he looked me in the eye and said "I'm disgusted with you." And with that, he turned and walked away.

I would have felt better if he had opted to crack me in the jaw, but I was acutely aware that Dad had never really vented at me, verbally or physically. At least the Band-Aid was ripped off and whatever indignities followed would pale in comparison to what I felt right then.

After an awkwardly quiet dinner we sat together on the two-foot-high, fifteen-foot-square concrete slab that served as our covered front porch. I sat on the edge shuffling my flip-flops in the dirt while Dad sat in a lawn chair nursing a beer and puffing on one of his trademark stinky cigars. I could have searched our five TV channels for something other than a summer rerun, but I felt compelled to stay close and serve my time in plain sight.

The problem was that the heat was just as stifling as the situation. While the torrential late summer rains were a few weeks away, the humidity of the monsoon season had arrived. In spite of the dark, we sat in heavy, triple-digit heat and watched lightning dance from the bellowing thunderheads that formed above the White Sand mountain range directly north of us.

Finally, looking for any form of relief, I asked Dad if I could take the old Cushman for a ride. He said, "Go ahead."

As always, the lumbering beast's big Briggs & Stratton engine fired up on the first pull. I hopped on, squared it up, and slowly scooted up our long driveway before turning left onto the paved road in front of our house. Did I mention that the headlight on the old scooter hadn't worked for years?

As crazy as that sounds, I should explain that moonlight-only rides on bikes, cycles, or whatever, weren't at all unusual. That speaks to just how remote our homestead was. We had our immediate neighbors a hundred yards to the west, but then you had to travel another mile down the road before you encountered the next house, which happened to belong to one of my mom's older brothers, Uncle Lloyd.

There was rarely any traffic, but in the event that there was, you had forever to get safely clear of it. While surrounded by the beautiful White Sands and Luna mountain ranges, the little valley we lived in was flat, so we could see car lights coming from miles away.

I had just checked my position near the white line on the right side of the road before I looked up at a particularly beautiful flash of lightning that struck as I approached my uncle Lloyd's place.

Four miles to the north was the ill-fated community of White Sands, and while closer, it was still barely in the shadow of its namesake mountain range. The initial idea for White Sands was brilliant—oversized lots sitting in the virgin desert north of the irrigation system. The problem was that for every buyer who envisioned a future Scottsdale, Phoenix' high-end neighbor to the east, there were those who opted to create their own private trailer parks, and the final group of the residents fell somewhere in between, including the Gates family.

Jeannie Gates was a sweet girl and my classmate; her big brother, Dick, was the same age as my brother, Doug. In spite of his generally goofy nature, Dick was an outstanding dirt bike rider, and that was what he had been doing for about an hour when I set out on the scooter. But there was a problem—Dick was five miles from home on a stripped down, off-road bike that was never equipped with lights.

He raced up the dirt road parallel to my uncle Lloyd's farm and slowed down as little as possible. Then he swung wide in a swooping turn to the right that carried him across both lanes of the road and directly into my path.

Without lights or the ability to hear one another coming above the roar of our own engines, we smashed head-on into each other in what qualified, by any standard of measurement, as the middle of nowhere.

From inside my uncle's house, my cousin heard the sound of smashing metal and engines popping out of gear and joked to her dad that Greg must have just crashed his motorcycle. Uncle Lloyd went out to the road to investigate, and that is exactly what he found. Apparently, I was walking about disoriented, but looked otherwise uninjured. I wasn't. And poor Dick, clad in a helmet, was writhing on the pavement acutely aware of the pain in his shredded hands and knees.

Uncle Lloyd got me in his pickup and rolled carefully down our long dirt drive. When we arrived, he told Dad, "I've got your boy here."

"You can't," Dad countered, "He just left…"

With that, I remember unlatching my door and tumbling to the ground. Uncle Lloyd and my dad helped me up and steadied me at each elbow, then ushered me in to my bed where I immediately drifted off to sleep. Uncle Lloyd then taxied the groaning Dick Gates back to his house and his parents promptly rushed him to the hospital.

The next morning I awoke and quickly decided it was worthless to try and sort out which part of me hurt worse. I tried to raise my head, but that proved so difficult I opted instead to lift my aching left arm into view, and while swollen beyond its normal diameter, it was at least free of blood. The same effort to view my right arm revealed missing chunks of flesh from my fingers and bright red abrasions that ran as far up my arm as I could see. The tight, dry pain throbbing throughout my shoulder suggested the damage reached well beyond my limited ability to view it. I managed a weak smile just the same, because the unmistakable work of my Dad's well-practiced first aid was in full evidence.

I gingerly pushed up onto my elbows and realized why my head was so hard to move. As I rose up, so did my pillow, now one with my hair by way of oozing, coagulated goo.

An hour later, Dad told Dr. Granite he would have never let me sleep it off if he knew a head wound was seeping somewhere beneath my stringy, longish hair. We stayed there for another hour as my cracked left arm received a full-length, white plaster cast from my armpit all the way down to my crooked fingers. Then, the doctor shaved my head so he could apply a tidy line of long overdue stitches to my wound.

I looked sympathetically at my poor dad and wondered if he remembered the last time we were there together. I was in the seventh grade and an errant bus driver's elbow had shattered the bridge of my nose during Mercury Elementary School's annual student/faculty basketball game. Dr. Granite attempted to straighten my broken nose before tilting my head toward Dad to ask, "How's this look?" I remember thinking Mom would disapprove no matter what he said, and she did when she realized my previously cute Martin nose, a feature from her side of the family, was history.

The next morning, we lit out bright and early for the family cabin in the mountains of central Arizona. We were quiet for a long time before I finally broke the silence and thanked Dad for lining up a great summer job for me. I realized that, with the cast on my arm, I couldn't wash dishes anymore, so I told him that it was fun while it lasted. That's when Dad corrected me with the first good news I'd had in days. He had told Amos and Audrey about my accident and they made it clear that they hoped I'd return to work for them in six weeks when the cast came off. Of course, my dishwashing job couldn't be held for me, but Amos was anxious to train me to take over as the new steak cook.

That news was so wonderful that I knew it would allow me to endure the tongue-lashing that Mom was going to unleash on me when she learned of my recent exploits. Amazingly enough, that never happened. I think Dad decided that karmic fate had already struck surely and swiftly and that I was clearly suffering enough. He decided not to tell her about the fallout that occurred from borrowing her younger brother's truck. A big softy at heart, Dad wouldn't wish six weeks of "I told you so" and "you're *only* fifteen" on anyone—not even me.

PROM AND PREJUDICE

A "DON'T DRINK AND DRIVE" PUBLIC SERVICE ANNOUNCEMENT

As the amateur historian and genealogist in my family, I have come to appreciate that otherwise right-thinking people could not help but be victims of their times, and as such, they may have embraced practices we might find unacceptable or even unconscionable today.

This is just one of the reasons I sometimes wince while writing casually about a misspent youth that featured more than its share of drinking and driving—a practice I would ultimately come to deplore for all the obvious practical and moral reasons. Strangely, I didn't feel that way in high school, nor did any of my classmates. Social drinking has always gone on and been common to city and country mice alike. Kids who carried on wildly in more urban settings faced their own, unique challenges, but, unlike us, they didn't have to traverse long narrow roads to get home from desolate party places.

Crashes were not uncommon, and sadly, neither were fatalities. I can easily recall the loss of half a dozen acquaintances during my four years at Deerville High—and one in particular that happened just prior to the fall prom of my junior year.

Things had been much improved for me up to that point. I was still impatient to get on with everything, having taken my driver's license road test in Mom's boat-like Plymouth Satellite station wagon. I had to use her car because its automatic transmission meant I could ace the test one-handed since my left arm was still encased in two feet of plaster. The instructor was so amused he mercifully allowed me to forego the ordeal of parallel parking, something I still stink at today.

I had a great job and then, finally, practical transportation: a windowless, 1965 Ford Econoline van-cum-party-mobile. Because I could decide how I came and went, I was no longer at the mercy of transportation happenstance. My newfound control allowed for a more reasoned approach to school, work, and social opportunities. I was having more fun than ever, but the appearance I gave off at home was of a more patient and mature sixteen-year-old. And since long hours at work made me scarce at home anyway, neither Mom nor I wanted a repeat of the bickering that resulted from the recklessness of my sophomore year.

All was well at The Bull Dogger steakhouse, too. Moving me from the sinks in the kitchen to steak cook at the massive exposed grill in the front of the dining room worked out to everyone's great satisfaction. The Emmons, however, seemed increasingly conscious of the fact that their prized employee was in high school and missed out on a lot in order to work long nights every evening but Monday. When, weeks in advance, I worked up the courage to ask for a Friday night off to attend the prom, their approval was immediate and coupled with palpable relief. I remember Amos slapping me on the back with such grinning gusto that I had to readjust my cowboy hat, a look-the-part concession to cooking on display in the dinning room.

With the stars lining up so perfectly, I worked up the further courage I needed to ask out a Deerville farm girl named Olivia Paulsen. A beautiful young sophomore, I assumed she was already on the short list of other guys who had known her since grade school. And, while I was not normally attracted to the blue-eyed-pom-pom-girl type, it wasn't only her appearance that interested me. Olivia was sharp, in a quiet, self-confident, and subtly funny way, and I was genuinely interested in getting to know her better. Having received one of those rare and intoxicating tips that the interest might actually be mutual, I asked if she was willing to tolerate me in the hideous shade of pastel that passed for prom tuxedo chic that season. Her smile expressed approval, but she cautioned that she was doubtful she could go, as her over-protective father didn't think she was yet old enough to attend prom. That stated, she thanked me for the invitation and asked for the opportunity to make her case to her dad.

Two days later, she approached me with a soft, easy smile and said, to her delight and genuine surprise, her father had agreed to let her attend prom with me. He had fond memories of my mother from their school days together and was sure he could trust his little girl with any son of Gayle Martin's. "Holy shit," I thought to myself, "no pressure in that."

Flattered, even my mom agreed to help by loaning me the use of what was only the second new car purchase of my parents' adult life together. My big brother, Doug, and I had our own rides and since the family of six no longer piled into just one car, they traded their massive Plymouth wagon for a shining white Mercury Monterey. Sure, it was a big, boxy, four-door sedan that accommodated the four little ones, but that made it all the more limo-esque as a prom night chariot.

There was one other motivating caveat in Mr. Paulsen's approval, but it was a most welcome one. Since prom dates are commonly multi-couple affairs anyway, I was only too happy to know we would participate in the event with Harlan David, another farm kid who was well-known and whose family was friendly with the Paulsens, and his date, Charlene Milano. She was an unusually sophisticated junior classmate, co-captain of the pom-pom line, and a mentor of Olivia's.

And that is how prom began—with so many things going so right. Then, something much more important went terribly wrong. Three of our classmates had been out drinking and the driver was handling his utilitarian pickup as if it were a nimble sports car. As they sped down the winding desert road, the driver remembered the limitations of his vehicle too late—and he slammed headlong into a telephone pole. He survived the crash, as did the kid riding shotgun. The boy in the middle, Max Fiori, was not so lucky. He was launched through the windshield and died amidst the shattered glass on the rumpled, steaming hood of the pickup. This occurred just three days prior to the big prom night.

As I sat tux-clad behind the wheel of the glistening new Mercury, Harlan and I discussed this sorry state of affairs as we drove toward what I thought was the Milano home to retrieve his date. Instead, he directed me to park near the pay phone at the end of the parking lot of Deerville's newer convenience store.

He then reached into his coat and produced the brown-paper-bagged bottle that was bulking up his otherwise smooth appearance. While a drink would have been expected under happier circumstances, that dark-colored hard liquor had an unmistakable "drown your sorrows" feel to it. Harlan had been on the phone with Charlene just prior to hopping into the car with me. She was really struggling and understandably on the fence about attending prom after all that happened. Even though she knew it was time for us to pick her up, she still wanted to think things through. We were to call her in just under an hour, and she'd spoken to my date who was happy to take her cues accordingly.

Harlan explained all this after taking a long pull on the dark brown bottle and handing it my way. As I paused and studied the bottle suspiciously, Harlan remembered my aversion to hard brown liquor. I did fine with clear alcohols, and respected their kick. I knew well why tequila was served in tiny shots, or why vodka was cut with tangy, diluting mixers that allowed you to manageably nurse it.

While it didn't appear so at the time, and while I was much more motivated out of selfish concerns for minimizing my own physical discomfort and preserving my personality, I was becoming a more responsible consumer of alcohol. Yes, never mind that I was behind the wheel. But I certainly had enough experience with drunkenness by then to know that I didn't like the loss of control common to any drinking that took me beyond a mild buzz. I enjoyed a good laugh, the true point of socializing with friends, and I had an appreciation for the verbal timing central to that. Slurring messed up such timely communication immensely. As for the pain of the dreaded hangover, I'd already subjected my young body to so much unintended physical discomfort that I saw no reason to compound it by intentionally doing so with an easily controllable substance.

This would have come as a major revelation to friends who rightly observed that my right hand was already permanently crooked into the shape of a twelve-ounce beer can. I wasn't, however, a complete hypocrite. I really enjoyed my beer, but by this time I was well aware of how to pace myself and I consumed it accordingly. That, and the fact that one of my worse bouts of drunkenness had come at the consumption of too much bourbon, were foremost in my mind as I continued to contemplate the bottle Harlan had handed me.

"Sorry," he interrupted. "I know you don't like the dark stuff, but this was handy and I promise you it will go down easy."

I sniffed the unmistakable fragrance of brandy. Not that it mattered, but since I didn't want to slip it from its protective brown paper sheath, my only question was to the exact nature of its fruity aroma. "Peach?" I inquired.

"Apricot," came Harlan's reply. And with that, I took a long, slow drink and felt the warm burn of the altogether tolerable liquor go all the way down to my stomach. It was the first of many passes of the bottle back and forth, and we were much more focused on our conversation than on our consumption.

We talked a lot about the fate of poor Max and how he would chuckle at the prospect of me and Harlan appearing dateless together as the cutest couple at the prom. We talked about the growing awareness of how unique he was, as well. His dad's job had deposited him into Deerville just two years earlier. An affable hippie, he was one of those guys who could talk to anyone about anything. He was also one of the few guys around school who didn't seem to care if anyone noticed his interest in girls was motivated more by laughing conversations and sharing inside secrets rather than the rampant pursuit of sex. The mutual admiration between him and girls like Charlene was envied by others, regardless of its motivation.

Harlan finally drained the last of the brandy, commented on the perfect timing, and exited my Mom's car for the pay phone. He sauntered back, looking much more himself and said simply, "We're on."

Given that we would arrive beyond fashionably late under the best of circumstances, a beautiful but resolved Charlene emerged from her family's high-end, low-slung ranch style home when she saw us pull into their long, circular driveway. That helped, because we still had to travel well west of town to the Paulsen farm to pick up Olivia.

Once in her home, I looked for Olivia's father so that I could deliver my well-rehearsed expression of appreciation and promise to take good care of his daughter before getting her home at a reasonable time...blah...blah...blah. He was nowhere to be seen, however, and that was a very good thing because, as I stood there watching Olivia's mom hastily apply the corsage to her daughter's wrist, I felt the swooning effects of the brandy suddenly sweep over me.

On the drive to the high school I admitted to the sudden rush I was struggling with, and my already sloppy speech was making my drunkenness pretty obvious anyway. Harlan paid attention, but the girls seemed too busy catching up to really notice what was happening.

I carefully maneuvered Mom's car into a space that, by our late arrival, constituted a lengthy walk to the entrance of the high school gymnasium. Any chance of the girls remaining oblivious to my rapidly deteriorating condition vanished when Olivia had to steady my gate at my left elbow while Charlene struggled to complement her efforts on my right. They employed all their pom-pom girl coordination to keep me headed in the right direction. I remember thinking how cool it would look to enter the gym flanked, as I was, by two of the prettiest girls in school. Yep, and that is the last thing I remember thinking.

I awoke face down with my right eye smashed closed on a surface just soft enough to qualify as something harder than a pillow. I eased open my left eye and recognized the pale sage-colored short shag of my parent's living room carpet. With my head throbbing, I rotated my eye enough to appreciate how the carpet clashed with my still tuxedo-clad, pastel blue shoulder. As I slowly rolled over, I was relieved to see no disappointed parents wondering why their teenager was passed out on the floor. Instead, I saw the dim amber light of daybreak creeping through the mercifully drawn window shades, which told me I was running out of time quickly. The little ones would spring from bed for the ritual of Saturday morning cartoon marathons at any moment.

It took only a second for my pain-induced self-pity to give rise to a far greater concern. Since I could not recall a single detail since I stumbled toward the decorated high school gym entrance, I had no idea how I arrived home. Worse, I didn't know anything about the place, nor the condition, of Mom and Dad's new car.

I eased to my feet and slipped out the front door as quietly as possible, hugely relieved to find the beautiful white Mercury in perfect condition parked just as it should have been. With that, I slipped back into the house, peeled out of what seemed like endless layers of punishing clothing, slipped into bed, and pulled my pillow squarely over my ears. I hoped to sleep, but if that failed, even lying perfectly still would help. A little while later, I got into the shower.

Perhaps the greatest challenge of being a sixteen-year-old with a crushing hangover is the obligation you have to conceal it and act as though you had a lovely evening the night before...lovely...simply lovely. While cold water washed over the back of my pulsing skull, I contemplated that demanding performance and the kind of missing but routine details I would be forced to fabricate. It was around ten in the morning and time to face the music, quite literally, and the noise of the TV, and all of the other commotion of a family of eight all together in the same space. I normally relished those mornings, but the only advantage the din afforded me on this particular day was the added cover of chaos.

Then I removed the towel from my shaggy wet hair, and I saw in the bathroom mirror that such casual cover was not going to be business as usual. Maybe it was the empty stomach, or the speed with which we had sucked down the sickening sweet apricot brandy—either way, the alcohol rush that had poisoned my body proved too much for a vessel on the inside of my right eye. The resulting burst left what should have been the white area around my iris flooded in a brilliant shade of crimson. Ultimately, the unsightly distraction proved somewhat helpful and made it unnecessary to seem overtly pleasant as my mom expressed concern and the younger kids took turns examining what they gleefully determined to be the perfect combination of cool and gross. I simply noted that my right eye was extra itchy on the drive home last night and that I must have unwittingly rubbed on it way too hard. I explained all this while I covertly slammed down the carbonated Coke I needed to keep my weakened body from visibly trembling.

A short while later, I stretched the extra-long but perpetually tangled cord of our kitchen phone out the back door and placed a call to Olivia. Her mother answered and I hoped I had not sounded too much like Eddie Haskell while speaking with her. Olivia came on the line after what seemed like a long time. I offered an apology and acknowledged that my drunkenness must have compromised her evening and waited for what I hoped would be her forgiving response, but it never came. After a few long quiet moments, I tried again. "Can you at least tell me what time I got you home last night?"

"You didn't," she replied. Then the phone went dead.

With increasing concern and urgency, I dialed up Harlan David's house. His always effervescent mother laughed that he had not emerged from under the covers yet and maybe I could try back later. Sure, I tried to respond casually, but inside I felt as though I was descending into some sick, private hell that only the great Alfred Hitchcock could appreciate. I was a young man in trouble who couldn't remember a thing.

My next call went to the Milano residence, and that call finally offered a bit of clarity on the unseemly details of my only great blackout-inducing escapade. It helped that Charlene herself answered and expressed relief to know that I called from the safety of my home. She tried to spare me further humiliation, but she made clear I had not been my usual sweet, funny self the night before. In fact, my condition eroded so quickly that they made arrangements for other, more responsible parties to escort Olivia home. Our budding courtship was over before it ever really got started. Charlene admitted also, that she used me as an excuse to exit the prom early—which she said her heart wasn't really into anyway. Harlan, amazingly, stayed to enjoy a raucous stag effort on his own after helping Charlene guide me to Mom's car so she could drive me back to her house to sleep it off. Worried to find me absent from her family's couch in the wee hours of the morning, Charlene thought I might still be too drunk to walk, let alone climb behind the wheel of my mom's car and drive myself all the way to my house, but that is exactly what I had done.

My return to school on Monday was met with plenty of commentary regarding my fame—or infamy—depending on whether the witness to my inebriation was an impressed fellow student or a concerned faculty member. For those who managed to miss the affair, the slowly browning mass that filled the inside of my right eye remained a month-long reminder.

I was lucky. With that, and with this important public service announcement about the stupidity of drunk driving behind us, I promise you can read on without having to endure further bouts of my guilt and self-reflection, except perhaps to offer one hopeful observation.

I write stories for a variety of reasons, but not the least of which is my belief that *someday* my kids deserve a complete picture of their father. Given that they have proven to be so much more enlightened and capable than I ever was at their ages, I trust that they'll show better judgment than I did. Better yet, I hope they turn out to be just like their mother.

CHICKEN QUICK DELIVERY

Even an old desert town can be a relatively new place in the broad scheme of things. Consequently, if one of these isolated burbs of faux civilization leaves something to be desired, one need only query the previous generation or two for clues to its dysfunction.

Deerville had the misfortune of being a mere hour down the road from a much larger cow town. After World War II, when the thrill-seeking set craved the white-hot excitement of movie houses, dance halls, and ice cream parlors, people perceived those things to be bigger and better in the city. Patronizing the local haunts was not fashionable. Those establishments failed, one by one, leaving Deerville commercially and culturally compromised.

By the time I was coming of age, Deerville was little more than a harbor of the bare necessities—the bank, our high school, the post office, and a couple of gas stations. Equally devoid of charm and personality was Gentry's Grocery Store, an oddball stop on my serpentine path of adolescent employment.

Competition for stock boy jobs at Gentry's was fierce, particularly among townies, that is, those kids who actually lived within walking or bicycling distance to the store. My family lived in the nothingness twelve miles beyond Deerville's ill-defined borders. This meant Mr. Gentry not only had to trust that I would *want* to come to work, but also that my state-of-the-ancient-arts automobile was dependable enough to get me there.

I put plenty of effort into convincing Mr. Gentry that my car and work ethic were equally sound, but I suspect the real reason he hired me had more to do with my older brother, Doug. Although he showed up on a regular schedule and received a paycheck, I never thought Doug so much *worked* at Gentry's as *appeared* there, much the way Cosby appears in Las Vegas. Doug figured out that, in Deerville, a place where unusual road kill was good for days of lively conversation, his role of class clown could be parlayed into something much bigger. That's just what Doug did; he became the biggest personality in Deerville, the smallest of venues.

In high school, the mind-numbing morning ritual of reading announcements over the intercom system rotated between class presidents until one morning when Doug filled in. He was never president of anything, but Doug became the Franklin Delano Roosevelt of announcements. He didn't relinquish the job until forced to by graduation. A few years later he was back at it, more or less, hosting his own morning show at the onset of his successful radio career.

Several times each year, our mild-mannered principal assembled the student body in the auditorium for any number of mundane reasons. Those occasions were more bearable when Doug came out first and warmed up the audience. After one such episode, a friend of mine elbowed me in the ribs and asked how my brother got that job. "Beats the hell out of me," I replied.

Doug's responsibilities at Gentry's were equally vague, but Mr. Gentry liked having him around. Perhaps it was because Doug wouldn't simply throw away an over-ripe cantaloupe; instead he would penetrate it with a firm green banana and pull back the peel to hide the puncture wound. Then he would fashion an official-looking sign that read, "Bananaloupes – 50 cents a pound." Admittedly, the people of Deerville were easily amused, but when Doug was "on" he was really quite funny. I once heard him get on the store intercom and turn "wet mop clean-up on isle five" into three minutes of strong comedy material. Mr. Gentry knew Doug was good for business.

When Doug moved along, Mr. Gentry hired me and hoped I would carry on the rib-tickling tradition. He managed to conceal his disappointment upon realizing I was much more Zeppo than Chico to my brother's Groucho Marx routine. I was, however, polite to the customers and exhibited at least average common sense, something that was in short supply among that season's crop of stock boys. For those reasons, I was rewarded with one of the better "kid" jobs Gentry's had to offer, that of assistant meat cutter.

If you can think of Gentry's as the Starship Enterprise, the meat department was the equivalent of the bridge. Our cutting room was situated at the back of the store, which was about half the size of today's grocery stores. We could be seen "trimming the fat fantastic" through two glass windows which ran the length of our refrigerated display cases. Inside the cutting room, a band saw separated two well-worn butcher blocks. A sink was in one corner, a slicer in the other, and our wrapper was on a small table near the windows. Whenever a customer buzzed for service, we slid the windows open and leaned out to help them. A carpet of loose sawdust covered the concrete floor except where the door to the walk-in cooler swept it clean. Inside the walk-in, quarters of beef hung from metal hooks that rolled on little wheels along a rail suspended from the ceiling. There were also lamb and pork products and waxy cardboard cases of chicken stacked three high, five deep.

The butcher, Fast Freddie Perez, was a knife-wielding mass of snarling fun. He worked at the store when Mr. Gentry bought it, and everyone assumed he would still be there when Mr. Gentry was long gone. Mr. Gentry spent most of his time in a small office in the stockroom, tending to the store's books. He occasionally came into the cutting room to make small talk with Freddie over a cup of coffee. When Freddie and I were alone again, I teased Freddie for calling Mr. Gentry "Boss." The preppy, urbanite store owner who commuted in from the city, was clearly intimidated by Freddie. We relished those unnecessary visits—they were good for hours of wise-cracking fun.

I can only recall one serious conversation in that cutting room, and it centered on me. While Freddie stood there with a dour look on his face, a fidgeting Mr. Gentry nervously explained that we had a problem. He explained that my work was aesthetically pleasing and that it prompted compliments from the likes of Mrs. Newton, who was considered the prettiest woman in Deerville in spite of being old enough to have two high school-aged daughters. But I was working too slowly and would have to pick up the pace a bit. I told Mr. Gentry and Freddie that I understood their concern, but that picking up the pace simply wasn't an option. I had plans of becoming a commercial artist and intended to leave their employ with all ten digits intact. Freddie seemed hurt to learn that I had no interest in following in his plodding, bloody footsteps. Mr. Gentry just stood there thinking. After a few awkward moments of silence, I offered to trade jobs with any stock boy interested in making this particular expression of the culinary arts his life's work. Always the merchant, Mr. Gentry considered the possible reaction of one of his biggest spending patrons and muttered, "No, Mrs. Newton might not understand." The subject of my productivity never came up again.

A few months later, a meat cutting exhibition of unprecedented speed and coordination took place at the site of that conversation. And I, of all people, anchored the endeavor.

It could only have happened on a Sunday, when Gentry's Grocery Store was at its dysfunctional best. For reasons I will never understand, Fast Freddie Perez and Mr. Gentry stayed home on Sundays. This left the inmates in complete control of the asylum. Without Freddie, I had no one to torment with practical jokes or challenge to games of "Name That Tune" using the store's Muzak system. Sundays were also the day that the Tastee Freeze called for a case of chickens to be restaurant cut. It was out of sheer boredom that I started executing that chore at break-neck, finger-threatening speed.

A restaurant cut involves passing a whole chicken through a band saw six times, yielding ten uninspired pieces of fowl. Legs and thighs turned out okay, but the carcass also got split up the middle, resulting in pieces comprised of half-back and half-breast. While this technique cut down on waste, it created cuts that were eerily indistinguishable. I usually added a seventh cut to remove the chicken's tail nub. I didn't want some little kid's self-esteem dashed by the certain knowledge that life, or in this case, Tastee Freeze, had clearly dealt them the chicken's butt. That's just the kind of guy I was.

Each week, I got faster, and the stock boys eventually figured out that I was always trying to beat my previous week's elapsed time for tearing through a case of twenty-four chickens. They got in on the act by seeing how quickly they could deliver the freshly cut birds to Tastee Freeze, halfway across town. After a few months of practice, we worked with the intensity of alley cats focused on an unwary rodent. We peaked with an effort that featured the precision and coordination of an Indy 500 pit crew and established the standard against which quick chicken cutting efforts will forever be judged.

Bill Vaughn was central to this effort as a participant and as an all-important facilitator. Bill was the store's assistant manager, which made him, not only the ranking kid in general, but the guy in charge on every adult-free Sunday. Mr. Gentry settled on him as Doug's successor. He was an excellent choice. A clipboard wielding, gum snapping bundle of energy, Bill had a well-earned reputation as a cool guy who inspired respect among the stock boys. While I didn't report to Bill, the rest of the crew did, and without his assistance, my absurd sideshow would have been without a supporting cast.

One of Bill's key contributions was authorizing the use of the company car. After a faded red Volkswagen Beetle sat idle in Gentry's customer parking lot for several days, one of the stock boys mentioned it to Bill. Of course, Bill didn't mention it to anybody. Instead, he assembled his crew and asked, "Do any of you know how to hot-wire a car?" They all raised their hands. "You guys are disgusting," Bill said, "I'm very proud of you." Then he laid down the rules. "We now have a company car. Any of you may use it during off hours, but I expect you to bring the car back in more or less the same condition it was in when you took it, and with more or less the same amount of gas."

Every Monday morning, the car showed plenty of evidence of extreme weekend use, but Bill said nothing until one morning when the bug wouldn't start. Someone had lifted the battery.

Bill assembled his crew again. "I try to make it easy for you guys. I treat you like adults and this is the thanks I get?" He continued to bark at them, "I don't *even* want to know who took the battery. But if it's not back by this time tomorrow, you'll all pay." Then he threw in some stuff Lee Marvin used on his troops in the *Dirty Dozen*. It was beautiful. The battery was back in the bug later that day.

The only other time I saw Bill go off on them was when Mr. Gentry tried one of his rare, non-food merchandising schemes. He placed a wire hamper on isle two filled with thermal underwear tops. The entire crew showed up wearing them the first Sunday after they went on display. "I don't care that you're all thieves," Bill yelled, "but I do care that you're all stupid! For God's sake, don't all wear them the same day. Some dumb-shit customer is going to tell Mr. Gentry that they just *love* the new uniforms!" Later that morning, Bill and I discussed how comfortable those damned tops were.

Rushing freshly cut chicken to Tastee Freeze in a company car offered another major advantage. While much of the ice that the chickens came packed in was lost when they were dumped unto the cutting board beside the saw, plenty of it still clung to the fleshy, semi-frozen birds. The waxy boxes they came in had holes strategically located to allow that melting ice and various other fluids to drain away. Using the company car to deliver dripping cases of raw chicken meant that no one had to get what we referred to as "chicken juice" on their own upholstery. It would get crazy stinky after a couple of days. That's probably why "chicken juice" never caught on as a breakfast drink.

To compensate for the VW's lack of speed, Bill assigned it to Lon Beckworth, the ultimate wheelman. Except for our common quest to move freshly cut chicken at the speed of light, I didn't hang much with Lon. He was a tall, lanky kid with stringy, blonde hair and horrible posture. Lon seemed to have an extra set of joints that allowed him to slouch even more than the rest of us. He was a "slacker" before there was a word for it and a nose miner extraordinaire. So relentless was his pursuit of desert-dried mucus that he rarely noticed the twisted expressions of those around him. He once told me, "Sure, anybody can pick something from their nose—the trick is in getting it back in." Then there was his prized collection of public restroom soap hair. Growing up out of town meant I was spared from Deerville Elementary School, so I asked one of his former classmates if Lon was always that goofy. He said, "No, he was pretty much normal right up until the circumcision." For reasons that were never explained, Lon wasn't circumcised until he was thirteen years old. About the only time Lon didn't seem crazy was when he was behind the wheel of a car driving much too fast. His family built and drove race cars. Lon was the real deal.

Finally, there was Charlie Trapp, my sawed-off little Mercury buddy, trusted ally, and "grunt" on our chicken quick delivery team.

It began like any other Sunday—the truck from Associated Grocers arrived at six in the morning. Bill and his crew, half of them quite hung over, were there to meet it. Over the next hour, they unloaded and checked invoices on the weeks' worth of inventory with virtually no adult supervision.

I showed up at seven, just ahead of the truck from Southwestern Meat Packing Company. I lined up the metal hooks on the ceiling-mounted rail that ran from the walk-in to the back door. Arthuro, a small man with the strength of Hercules, hoisted quarters of beef from his shoulder up to the waiting hooks. Each time he turned back toward his truck, I winced at the greasy shine of his right ear and the bits of tallow that mingled in his curly black hair. I didn't know what Arthuro got paid, but I was certain it wasn't enough.

After guiding the suspended sections of beef into the walk-in, I entered the cutting room. The stock boys were hungry that morning. The first thing they did upon arrival each Sunday was to turn on the hot pad portion of the meat wrapper, and then they would cruise the isles of Gentry's for breakfast food. That morning, a buffet of Vienna Sausages, Hostess Fruit Pies, and SpaghettiOs was balanced carefully on the hot pad's fabric-lined surface.

I surveyed the meat case and spent the next few hours replenishing those items that were in short supply. Then, the side door to the cutting room suddenly flew open and the room fell dark. I was glad I was tying a rump roast rather than handling a knife, but either way, sudden darkness was usually a good thing. On this occasion, it meant Mrs. Newton was headed for the meat department.

Turning off the lights made our sliding glass windows work like two-way mirrors. We could see out, but the customers couldn't see in, and this gave us the opportunity to observe the lovely Mrs. Newton without her being any the wiser. I looked up, expecting to see Charlie, but he was stuck up front bagging groceries for Bill. Lon and two other stock boys huddled in anticipation as Mrs. Newton leaned over the display case, causing her boat neck blouse to gape open before them. She flipped through the Styrofoam trays, searching for the best cuts of beef. Her efforts resulted in a magnificent display of undulating cleavage.

The telephone rang, causing the hair on my neck to stand up. I glanced over at the wall phone and saw that the button for line one was glowing, which meant Bill had answered it up front. It was probably nothing.

Mrs. Newton straightened up and one of the stock boys said in a hushed tone, "There they are." Leaning over the refrigerated display case always had that effect on Mrs. Newton. "Nature's thermometers just kicked in," Lon added.

Bill worked the cash register with one hand and pressed the phone to his ear with the other. He was speaking to Ernie, a transplant from the Midwest and proprietor of Deerville's Tastee Freeze franchise.

"Hey Bill, we could sure use a case of chicken over here," Ernie said.

"Sure thing, Ernie. How soon would you like it delivered?" asked Bill.

"Pretty quick," came Ernie's reply.

Sounding like Clint Eastwood delivering a catch phrase from one of his hard guy movies, Bill couldn't resist asking slowly and deliberately, "Chicken quick?"

Like an apron-clad, three-headed monster, the stock boys shuffled in unison to the next window. Mrs. Newton was here, hovered over the pork section.

The store's intercom system popped and hissed before Bill uttered three words that set off a frenzied explosion of activity. "Chicken quick delivery."

I instinctively hit the light switch. Mrs. Newton's eyes bulged and her mouth fell open as the cutting room lights burst on, illuminating the crimson faces of three horrified stock boys. They were cheek to cheek, just inches from Mrs. Newton's heaving bosom.

By the time I swung the band saw into position, Charlie had already sprinted up aisle one, and before the blade was spinning at cutting velocity, he had dumped a case of chickens onto the cutting block to my right.

Bill kept Ernie engaged in conversation a moment longer, hoping to minimize the time between Ernie hanging up his phone and one of us buzzing at his delivery door.

I reached for the first pale, icy carcass, wings in my left hand and legs in my right, and began to cut. Kerry held the now empty cardboard case just in front of me and to my left. I flipped the severed pieces of chicken in his general direction without having to focus my eyes there.

Lon Beckworth grabbed the screwdriver that doubled as an ignition key and loped through the stockroom like a giraffe trying to elude Marlin Perkins on *Mutual of Omaha's Wild Kingdom*. He ducked out the back door and angled up the alley toward the parking lot and the company car.

I ripped through chickens at an eight-second clip. Sorry kids, no time for tail trimming today. I've got a record to beat.

Above the hum of the band saw, we heard Bill bark out instructions in the stockroom. "Clear a path in here! Damn it, men, we've got chicken comin' through!"

As I reached for the last chicken with my right hand, I felt my left thumb hit the saw blade. It didn't hurt, but bad cuts rarely do at first. This was before the AIDS epidemic made everyone squeamish about other people's bodily fluids, but it was still poor form to bleed on someone's extra crispy picnic sampler. Whatever the damage, assessing it would have to wait another eight seconds. I flung the last two pieces of chicken toward Charlie and grabbed for the box lid. I got just a glimpse of his face, spotted with tiny specks of twisted pink flesh—the chicken equivalent of sawdust. I secured the lid atop the case and Charlie spun on his heels and out the cutting room's side door which Bill had propped open on his way to the back.

I raced after him, but even maneuvering a case of chicken, he sped away from me. Charlie sprinted out the store's backdoor and into the alley where he hurled the waxy cardboard box onto the passenger seat of the revving Volkswagen.

Bill was there to close the bug's door, but he never got the chance. Lon, folded up behind the wheel of the tiny car, dumped the clutch and sped away. The bug's door slammed flush to the cab from the force of Lon's acceleration. We watched in awe as the company car built speed down two alley blocks before he negotiated a hard right turn without ever setting off the brake lights.

As my adrenaline slowed, I remembered my thumb. It already sported a Band-Aid from a small cut to its side earlier that day. The band saw blade cut neatly through the Band-Aid, but didn't break the skin.

A few minutes later, the phone rang. It was Ernie. He thanked Bill for anticipating his needs and having the chicken cut in advance. "I never got service like this in Des Moines," he said appreciatively.

"Well Ernie, thank God you're not in Ohio anymore." Bill grimaced as he hung up the phone. "I'm not sure he knew I was kidding."

A mere six minutes and thirty-eight seconds passed from the time Ernie called until we delivered the goods. We never bettered that time. For one thing, we lost Lon. He was already on probation for picking his nose in front of the customers when I hit the lights and scared the hell out of Mrs. Newton. Mr. Gentry decided to let him go. I blame myself.

A few days later, a nice highway patrolman came around asking Bill about the faded red VW Beetle. Seems one had been stolen in California a couple of months earlier. "Come to think of it," Bill said, "I guess that car has been sitting here for a while. Stolen you say?"

Like my brother before me, I moved on from Gentry's, trading it in for an easier coach's assistant job that I could ease into my schedule before reporting to work at The Bull Dogger each evening. Still, I was always grateful for the experience.

A few years later, I heard there had been an accident of some kind and Gentry's Grocery Store burned to the ground. I don't know for sure, but I would bet a case of chickens that it happened on a Sunday.

THEY CALL
THE WIND PARIAH

If you are put off by adventures involving bodily functions, you should read no further. Even though this particular function is the most harmless and, at times, the most amusing of social miscues, the horrific intensity of this particular episode should remind us all to remain ever-vigilant.

Your grandparents probably called it "wind." Your parents may have boldly called it "passing gas." I will refrain from using the most common term for it today, a term that prompts giggles from children of all ages. But you know what I'm referring to.

While the vast majority of these occurrences are innocent in nature, I urge you again to exercise caution, as the consequences can be serious.

John, my youngest brother, engaged in recreational flatulence and routinely sent my family running from the house, hoping to avoid his genuinely unpleasant, but not actually life-threatening, smells. Yet John told me that, on one occasion, he was dove hunting alone in the desert when he unleashed a demon of such paint-peeling fury that several birds fell from the sky without him firing a shot. He explained that he is usually immune from his own putrid emissions, even when they make others vomit. On this occasion, however, he claimed to have lost consciousness. He said that by the time he woke up and staggered back to his truck, the sun was setting. John said it was the most radiant shade of crimson he had ever seen.

Given that flatulence is a source of pride for John, I assumed he was exaggerating, although I was very glad not to have been there to find out. A short time later, I survived an experience that convinced me John may well have been telling the truth.

It was mid-January during my junior year in high school. I was driving my date, Terry Sanderson, and two other couples in my fixed-up utility van to a triple-billed concert of Johnny Rodriguez, Emmy Lou Harris and Asleep at the Wheel. Granted, we were from the sticks miles west of the city, but an event of this cultural significance could lure us into town.

Dinner had gone well enough, the concert was great, and we were headed home. Terry and I were in the front of the van, and my friends were in the back behind the curtains that separated the cab from the human cargo area.

That is when I sensed it. It wasn't so much a smell at first, just an uneasiness which alerts you that something is not right. These things always come as unpleasant surprises when they're not of your own doing.

At first I suspected my van. The front bucket seats were separated by a metal compartment that covered the engine. I sniffed for mechanical miscues—an over-heated motor, smoldering electric wires, and melting rubber hoses all offered unpleasant smells. It was none of those things, however, and I became increasingly aware that this unwelcome odor was human.

In short order, I realized what happened. It had to be Terry. This was such a bad one that if it originated in the back of the van there would surely have been a commotion.

"Wow!" I thought. "This is way worse than bad." Any thoughts of rolling around with Terry after dropping off the others quickly vanished. She was a nice girl, however, and I felt obliged to get past this thing without causing her unnecessary embarrassment.

"Good God!" I thought, "This could not be human!" Things were happening very quickly and I fought the urge to panic. I glanced in Terry's direction and noticed her legs were crossed and clinched conspicuously tight. "Too late for that," I thought.

I tried to remember my childhood prayers. I decided not to fill my lungs with fouled air, hoping to hold my breath until this monster passed. I assumed it was peaking and could not possibly get worse. Bad decision, but gulping in the nasal nightmare at that point would have caused me to hurl all over the windshield. Short, shallow breaths were my only hope—just enough air to retain consciousness.

I was feeling light-headed, not completely in control of my thoughts. I flashed back to the restaurant. We had not allowed the extra time necessary to dine at an establishment worthy of cloth napkins and subsequently had to rush through dinner. What had Terry ordered—macacha beef? Had she chewed it at all?

It seemed as though my chest was going to explode. I remember trying to convince myself that I could draw air in through my ears.

A strange pall fell over the vehicle. The talking and laughter so common to the back of the van had ceased. Is this what a troubled airliner sounds like when its passengers realize their fate rests entirely in the hands of their pilot? I wondered if the silence was due to the fact they were already dead.

I told myself to get a grip. I could not let six budding lives end in order to spare one young woman the embarrassment of acknowledging that she had spawned the anti-Christ of social indiscretions.

Even though the night air that enveloped our poisoned vessel was a crispy 40 degrees, I casually cranked down my window. At 70 miles per hour, the wind chill was paralyzing. It was not until I felt ice forming on my face that I realized my cheeks were streaked with tears.

The life-restoring wind whipped the curtains behind my head. In my rearview mirror, I caught surreal glimpses of pale, twisted faces, distorted by the most violently flared nostrils anyone has ever seen.

None of us ever spoke of what happened that night. I suspect it was just too painful.

I saw Terry again at our ten year high school reunion and was surprised to find her alive. I had assumed a body that harbored a gas of such vile toxicity must surely be compromised, yet she seemed to be in reasonably good health.

It was a bit difficult to carry on a conversation from a distance of twenty-five feet, but I think she understood.

THE BIRDS AND THE BEES—AND A COW

The single most important aspect of real estate investing also applies to the awkward art of coming of age—location, location, location. I say this because where you live when you're going through adolescence has a great deal to do with how the experience unfolds. Mindful of this, I always believed that guys from crowded Brooklyn neighborhoods had more in common with young villagers in Ethiopia than they did with me. In spite of major cultural differences, kids from both environments lived in communal settings and had an opportunity to at least observe members of the opposite sex, if not interact with them.

It was different growing up in the thinly populated desert Southwest. There, I had more in common with a teenaged boy tending his flock in the remote Basque hill country than I did with young Brooklynites. The primary difference was that I stayed in one place and didn't have easy access to attractive, young sheep.

Like most kids growing up south of the canal system that separated the raw desert from a matrix of cotton, safflower, and alfalfa fields, our nearest neighbors were often miles, rather than yards away. To be clear, however, we did have, by rural standards, what qualified as next door neighbors. About one hundred yards west of our home was the ancient farmhouse of Mr. and Mrs. Seth Reinhardt, but since they were even older than my grandparents, the dynamic of living completely free of kids outside my immediate family remained.

I liked the Reinhardts. The old man was tall, lean, and slightly bent. His hair, his hand-painted, vintage Chevy pickup truck, and his right eye were all the same shade of pale gray. The color of that eye was owed to exposure to chemical gas used on the battle fields of WWI. While Mr. Reinhardt was active and visible, his bed-ridden wife was rarely seen outside the home. Mom used to make extra helpings of food and send me or one of my brothers to deliver it "next door." Mrs. Reinhardt took as much pleasure in seeing us kids as she did in receiving Mom's culinary treats. The routine was always the same: Mrs. Reinhardt tried to give me a reward of small change, usually a dime. Per Mom's instructions, I refused payment. Mrs. Reinhardt then absolutely insisted, and I finally folded the coin into my tanned, little hand, ensuring the outcome everyone wanted in the first place.

The Reinhardts grew older as the years rolled by and I grew up a bit. Then, just as I was entering high school, Mrs. Reinhardt passed away. A few months later, Mr. Reinhardt sold his property and moved to Mesa, Arizona to live with an adult son I never knew existed.

By spring, the small farm that had slowly fallen into disrepair was in new hands, six of them to be exact, belonging to Ed and Alice St. James and their daughter, Sierra.

Soon I was busy with summer jobs, and with what little time I had to observe the St. James family, I found the patriarch, Ed, to be the most interesting. A big man, Ed St. James was a plumbing contractor from Phoenix who moved west to pursue the life he always wanted—owning and operating a small family farm. He wasn't as idealistic as Oliver Douglas on the TV show *Green Acres*, and rural Mercury probably wasn't quite as sophisticated as Hooterville. Out early and up late, Ed worked way too hard to be considered a real farmer. The real farmers I knew were portly fellows who drove around in air conditioned pickup trucks keeping tabs on an army of sinewy, sun-ripened Latinos who did the hardest of the farm work.

Mrs. St. James was no more evident than Mrs. Reinhardt had been, but her daughter, Sierra, was a common sight. She had long, skinny legs and brown hair in a bobbed cut. Though she was less than two years younger than me, Sierra reminded me of a young giraffe loping around the property whenever her dad was outside doing his thing.

As a teenager, I had less time and less reason to pay attention to the St. James family than I had as a little boy with the Reinhardts. They were simply there—close enough to see, but too far away to hear.

A year or so later, the benign side show that had been playing out in my peripheral vision got a new star. Little Sierra was not so little any more. Her legs were just as long, but they were now golden tan and boasted lovely curves; in fact, lovely curves graced her figure from head to toe. And that little girl hairdo had given way to a surfer girl mane of flowing, sun-bleached, caramel-colored hair. Ed's resurrection of the run-down little farm seemed in direct proportion to the blossoming of his daughter, and the girl I had previously viewed with disinterest became an increasingly interesting distraction.

Throughout my junior year, Sierra was a welcome sight around the campus of Deerville Union High School, and while my unique class schedule made such opportunities uncommon, I did give her the odd ride to or from school in my infamous 1965 Ford Econoline Van. Of course those occasions presented an opportunity for me to admire Sierra's statuesque figure up close, but her face was lovely, too. More country girl than Cover Girl, the term "brilliant smile" applied as much to her laughing eyes as it did to her big, white teeth. But laughing was the real attraction Sierra held for me. The girl had a wicked sense of humor, and that was the quality that tempted me into flirting with her.

For me, flirting was a fun and generally harmless way of interacting with an interesting girl. It wasn't something I necessarily did as a come-on, and it was fine with me if these engagements never went beyond verbal horseplay.

It was during one such ride-to-school conversation that Sierra asked me about my burdensome work schedule. She was generally aware that my job flipping hunks of dead red at The Bull Dogger Steakhouse meant working from 5 p.m. to 11 p.m., Tuesday through Sunday nights. She wondered how I maintained my reputation as a patron of the extracurricular arts with such a demanding weekly routine. I explained that The Bull Dogger itself sometimes presented opportunities for dancing on the canal bank after closing time, but that otherwise, I simply joined whatever parties Friday and Saturday nights had to offer fashionably late. Then I volunteered that with late spring weather making for lovely late-night temperatures, I sometimes laid out after work, deepening my moon tan.

Sierra wanted to know more, so I explained that I was still usually wide awake upon returning home from work, and that laying out under the night sky was a wonderful way to wind down. She got that, but wanted to know more about the moon tan part.

"That's easy," I said. "The light bouncing off a desert moon on a clear, cool night is so bright that you can actually tan under it. In fact, when the moon is full I have to be careful not to stay out too long so as not to get a moon burn."

Sierra's delight at the idea of moon tanning made me glad that I was able to conjure up such nonsense on the fly. Then she did me one better. "I want to try it," she said. "Are you going out tonight?"

Whoa. Verbal jousting was one thing, but maintaining your cool in the face of a most unexpected proposition from such a sweet and unexpected source required real concentration. Once I was sure I wasn't going to veer off the road and crash into the big, stinky Donaldson stockyards, I managed a response. "Yeah," I said, "tonight would be great, but you're sure 11:15 won't be too late?"

"11:15 is perfect," Sierra replied, "my folks will be sound asleep by then."

Suddenly, I was one up on the sheep herding kid from the Basque hill country.

The clock on the dining room wall of The Bull Dogger seemed out of whack that evening. No matter how many times I checked its progress against that of my watch and the clock in the bar, they all seemed to grind forward at a begrudgingly slow pace. Finally, mercifully, 11 p.m. arrived. Fortunately, it was a Thursday night and no patrons arrived late. I was in my van and headed home by thirty seconds past eleven.

On the ten minute drive home, I wondered about running in to take a quick shower, but decided against it since that wasn't my usual pattern of behavior and I didn't want to risk waking my parents or siblings. Besides, the smoky aroma of charred beef seemed to work as an aphrodisiac on some women.

By eleven past eleven I was strolling across the dirt equipment yard that separated our property from the St. James house. To my slight surprise and absolute delight, Sierra was waiting to greet me by the wire gate at the corner of their non-landscaped front yard.

I was relieved that we didn't get stuck in the small talk that can sometimes make initiating a first move awkward. Before I knew it, we were locked in a nice, long kiss. Immediately afterward, Sierra apologized for her poor technique. "What, are you crazy?" I asked. "That was quite nice."

"You're just being sweet," she countered, "I don't have any real experience. I don't even know how to French kiss."

"Well, neither do I," I lied, "but I've read enough about it to give it a try."

"You're so full of shit," she laughed, and then we went at it a while longer. Then for the first time since kissing Sierra hello, I began to think, "What time is it? How far is this likely to go? Does either one of us want it to go that much further right now? And if we do, where should we go?" A tryst on farm equipment could be fun, but required a familiarity and coordination not common to first encounters.

I couldn't help but wonder how Sierra would react if my hands tried to roam, but I decided against finding out. There didn't seem to be a reason to rush. Sierra slept just a hundred yards away. She wasn't going anywhere anytime soon, and neither was I. This was a uniquely convenient situation and I wanted to enjoy it. When we came up for air, I took the opportunity to pull back enough to look at my watch and ask, "Same time next week?"

Sierra didn't answer right away. Her expression didn't register relief or disappointment. Instead, she seemed to give my question serious consideration.

"Shit!" I thought to myself, "Have I blown it? Was it possible that she was thinking about opting out of a game that had been wonderfully fun to this point?" Outside I tried to maintain a James Bond cool, but inside I was quaking like Deputy Barney Fife.

She finally responded. "Next week would be great, but can we meet Friday night instead of Thursday night?"

My inner Fife just messed up his hair in excitement, but my outer Bond tried to look casual and said, "Friday is perfect."

With that, she grabbed my face with both hands, gave me a quick kiss, turned, and trotted toward the front door of her house. Then she stopped and called back to me "Don't forget your moon tan lotion."

Maybe I had played it okay after all. Either way, my lunar liaisons with Sierra were the most exciting things happening in a school year that was quickly and quietly drawing to a close.

Given our vastly different class schedules, I could go days without seeing Sierra around the high school. Still, the following week I kept an eye out for her, and when we passed within sight of one another, she was quick to offer a friendly wave and to smile her usual sunny smile. Her smile may have been a bit more knowing than before, or perhaps I just imagined that it was, but either way, it was reassuring to have some contact between encounters. I went about the business of the next week with the smug satisfaction of someone who knew something that no one else was in on except for the mesmerizing Sierra. I could hardly wait for Friday night to arrive.

Friday and Saturday nights were by far the busiest at The Bull Dogger Steakhouse. As busy weekends went, this particular Friday night was proving all together manageable. The dining room was empty by 10:15, and at 10:30, I went into the kitchen to freshen up with a small stack of wet paper towels.

Gus Hecht eyed me suspiciously. Gus was one of the smartest guys I knew, yet even with our senior year still ahead of us, it was already apparent that he would never accumulate enough credits to graduate on time. Gus was a legend in auto shop and industrial arts classes, but he rarely showed up for math, science, or English. Still, he was smart enough to know, with one look, what I was up to.

Amos and Audrey Emmons always hired a honky-tonk band to play in the dance hall portion of their establishment on Friday and Saturday nights. Normally, by this time on a weekend evening, Gus and I would have compared notes on which of the unattached women at the bar might be interested in the young charges of the steakhouse. Gus was easily better looking than me, but he was required to dress as his station of dishwasher dictated. I, however, was conspicuously positioned at the open flame grill in front of the dining room, so my ensemble of cowboy hat, western shirt, snug jeans, boots, and a holstered six-shooter helped level the playing field between us.

"You bastard," Gus protested, "you found a date for the canal bank before I could even break away from the kitchen?"

"Sorry, Gus," I replied. "I didn't notice anyone interesting in there, but you're welcome to whoever turns up. I'm calling it quits early tonight."

"You lying shack of shit," Gus challenged. "You couldn't wait to get home to brush your teeth?"

"Like I said," I smiled back at him, "I'm turning in early and just want to get a jump on things."

I strolled back into the dining room and leaned on the little wood corral that afforded me the space I needed around the grill for my tong-twirling exploits. I studied the dining room clock. The last table had been bussed clean almost an hour ago, and my mesquite wood fire had burned down to coals. With just fifteen minutes more until closing, however, it didn't seem as though it would matter.

That's when I heard the big, booming, slightly slurred voice of Ray Jagger. "Not Ray Jagger!" I thought. "F-word, F-word, F-word! Not Ray Jagger!"

Ray was not quite of average height and was well less than average weight. He had an olive complexion and his moon-shaped face was rimmed by short, black hair. Ray only came in the restaurant about every six weeks, but when he did, he always ordered dinner right at closing time. In fact, he sometimes announced to Audrey that he would not order until five or ten minutes after closing, and she always insisted that we accommodate Ray with a smile.

One reason for Audrey's flexibility was that Ray always treated numerous guests to dinner, offering them heaps of everything our menu had to offer. Not only that, he ran up famously huge bar tabs. Fortunately for me, the options of what could be thrown on the grill were limited to just a few different cuts of beef.

With my fire all but gone, I raced out the back door of the kitchen to grab a couple of mesquite logs off the wood pile. Just before the door slammed behind me, I heard Gus laugh, "Don't worry, I'll moisten some more paper towels for ya!"

It was nearly disastrous to have Ray parachute in late on this, of all evenings, but I was well aware that it could have been much worse. For one thing, Ray staggered in at a quarter until eleven, not a quarter past. Secondly, he was only playing host to a party of four, not his usual six or seven.

I pulled every trick I knew to hasten the grilling of their steaks despite knowing that, if I took longer, Ray would drink more and be less likely to notice if his steak was too red. The two couples in his court were not as lit up as Ray, but if their steaks were not to their liking, their embarrassment at having crashed the kitchen at closing muted their complaints.

At twenty past eleven, Audrey finally delivered the check. Ray could finally make a big show of paying the tab, then I could help Gus clear the table and slip away with a clear conscience. Since this wasn't a school night, I hoped that arriving a half-hour late to Sierra's house would be a forgivable offense.

Things were not going to go that smoothly, however. One of the gentlemen in Ray's party grabbed the check. This happened sometimes, but usually, after Ray insisted that they hand the check over—often at the top of his lungs—his shocked dinner guests capitulated. Not so with this big, burly fellow. He was not so easily intimidated. No matter how much Ray yelled, or how much he swore, the big bruiser just kept smiling and waddled slowly toward Audrey who stood nervously behind the cash register. I made a point of staying well away from the fracas out of genuine concern that Ray would pull the vintage Colt 45 from my holster and demand the check at gunpoint.

No one had ever picked up a check in Ray Jagger's presence, and we all knew we were entering unchartered territory. That's when the red-faced Ray screamed, "If you don't give me that goddamned check I'm gonna flip this fuckin' table over!"

Gus and I snapped looks of shocked amusement at one another. Ray's large friend paused just long enough to look at Ray like he couldn't possibly be serious and then continued his casual march toward Audrey.

Amos Emmons had made the tables at The Bull Dogger Steakhouse picnic-bench style from 2"x6" pine. Atop the red and white checked table cloth that adorned this particular table was an assortment of clear plastic water tumblers, empty long-neck beer bottles, beige plastic salad bowls, and five, heavy, stoneware dinner platters trimmed in mint green. With eyes bulging from his enflamed face, perspiration beading on his generous forehead, and veins swelling from his skinny neck, the wiry little madman gripped the edge of the table with both hands and sent it flying upside down. Gus could hardly contain his glee at the spectacle of it all.

Audrey's right eye started to twitch as the big man paid the bill. Ray flew from the restaurant shouting a stream of profanity, and I scurried about helping Gus collect the far-flung pieces of dinnerware. Gus glanced at me and said, "Get out of here already. I can sweep this mess up faster than I can wash it anyway."

"Thanks!" I said. And I raced for the parking lot and my trusty van. It was almost midnight before I swerved around our long rectangular driveway and trotted toward the now familiar meeting place at chateau St. James. The cleaning up I did before the mad dash to feed crazy Ray Jagger was for naught, but I thought maybe I could come up with a clever angle for the pitiful way I presented. "Heck," I thought, "maybe the irrigation ditch is running and we can go for a dip."

As I rounded the last obstacle in the gauntlet of the nearly antique farm equipment that stood silently between our houses, disappointment slowed my hopeful trot to a stop. In the pale blue moonlight, a full twenty-five yards from the little wire gate, it was clear that Sierra, the sensuous sentry, was not at her post. I certainly couldn't blame her. I was a full forty-five minutes late.

With nowhere else to go and nothing better to do, I continued to slowly shuffle toward the gate. While I hadn't felt that way the week prior, at that moment I felt exposed and vulnerable, like a trespasser.

"Greg!" Sierra called out in a hushed tone, "over here."

I squinted in the direction of the St. James house where I could just make out Sierra's tall silhouette in the shadows near the front door. Carefully opening the gate, I noticed for the first time that it squeaked. I then walked across the dirt front yard as quietly as possible. I reached the front of the simple house and saw Sierra standing in the threshold with the door half-opened behind her. Once I was close enough, Sierra reached out to put her hand on my shoulder and said, "I thought you'd never get here."

"Sorry," I said. "But I got held up at The Bull Dogger."

"Held up?" Sierra exclaimed.

"No, no," I explained, "not like a robbery or anything, just a crazed customer who got angry and flipped over a table full of dishes."

"What?" inquired Sierra with that glowing smile spread across her face.

It was clear she wanted to hear the details, and while conversation was not what I'd shown up expecting, I was happy to elaborate. Sierra looked as alluring as ever and it wouldn't hurt me at all to just enjoy the moment and gather myself a bit while recounting the craziness of the past hour.

Suddenly, I was struck with the serendipitous nature of life and how, in an instant—in the fraction of a second it takes to flip on a light switch—your sweetest dream can turn into your worst nightmare. That's what happened. In the house somewhere behind Sierra, a light bulb burst to life.

I already knew about the fight or flight instincts programmed into animals. Growing up in a rural setting, I had seen it play out plenty of times, but I never truly understood it until that moment. I was gone in a heartbeat. I didn't bother with the gate. Instead, I made a beeline for the three-foot-high fence around their yard and hurdled it at a speed that would have made my old track coach grin at this stop watch.

I rushed through the private entrance to my room at the corner of our house, knelt in the darkness, and peered out my window, waiting for the hulking profile of Ed St. James to come stomping into view. But he never came. When my breathing and heartbeat returned to normal, I rolled into bed and stared up into the darkness. Only then did it occur to me that, perhaps, I had acted cowardly. There were options to running I did not consider until that moment, but it was too late to go back now. Even if I did rush back, what would I do—tell Ed the Giant to spare his lovely daughter and instead grind my bones to make his bread? Whatever was going to happen to Sierra had already happened by that time. And, I figured, whatever consequences awaited me were apparently on hold until the next day.

It took me a long time to fall asleep and a long time to finally wake up. By the time my eyes focused on the clock by my bed, it read half-past noon. "Wow," I thought, "Ed St. James must be a sadistic bastard. Why didn't he just come roaring into our house and get it over with?"

In spite of my guilt around whatever unpleasantness Sierra experienced, I remained inside and out of sight. By four o'clock that afternoon I had showered, donned my steakhouse costume, and navigated my van out of our long driveway as inconspicuously as possible. Everything at the restaurant went normally that Saturday night. Gus was still so wound up about Ray Jagger's meltdown the night before, and the fact that he had sheepishly come in early that morning to pay for any damages, that he didn't notice how subdued I was.

On Sunday, I spent a lot of time in my room watching the St. James house for clues as to what might have happened Friday night. But all appeared normal. Ed fed animals and was on and off of tractors. Sierra ventured out briefly on a couple of occasions and looked none the worse for wear.

I stalked the places where I usually saw Sierra when I got to school on Monday, but I never saw her. By Tuesday morning, I was crazy with guilt and concern. Finally, in a break between late morning classes, I spotted her. I rushed toward her, and before she knew what was happening, I gushed about how sorry I was and how badly I felt.

Sierra looked at me with a mix of surprise and confusion. "Slow down, Greg," she said. "What are you talking about?"

"I'm so sorry I ran off Friday night." I stated. "I hope you didn't get into too much trouble."

Looking genuinely puzzled, she asked, "In trouble for what?"

"The light came on and I just assumed your dad…"

Sierra laughed a little and said, "So that's what happened to you. My dad didn't catch us, Greg. He sleepwalks to the bathroom every night about that time. He didn't even know we were out there."

According to Shakespeare, "A coward dies a thousand deaths." I died a few times myself that morning.

For the rest of the day, and all night at work, I tried to sort out what happened. Sierra didn't get caught, she wasn't in trouble, and she didn't even seem put off by my cut-and-run tactics. Suddenly, my priorities seemed clear. I needed to get the moonlight express back on track with Sierra.

Gone was my laid back attitude about letting things casually play out with the farmer's daughter next door. There was only one problem. We had initiated our dangerous liaisons at Deerville High, and the next abbreviated school day would be our last until classes resumed at the end of summer.

When the half-day of school on Wednesday didn't present any opportunities to see Sierra, let alone make a next date with her,

I found myself a man desperately in need of a plan. To the knowledge of Ed and Alice St. James, I had never set foot on their property. If I knocked on the door or rang the phone, they might get suspicious since they hardly knew I existed. No, all I needed was some uncomplicated way to connect with Sierra. If we happened to be outside at the same time, maybe we could simply point skyward and give each other the thumbs up. That would be enough to confirm that another moon tanning session was in the offing.

If I needed to wash my van, I knew it made most sense to do it in the shade of the backyard, before or after the mid-day sun had done its thing. But girl obsessed boys are rarely sensible. Around 11 a.m., I pulled my already clean van into an open, sunny spot in our front yard, which put me in easy view of anyone moving about the St. James property.

My practical car washing attire of rubber flip-flops, cut-offs, and a well-worn undershirt offered certain advantages. I hoped the bright sunlight playing on the misty overspray that settled on my shoulders would enhance the impression that my skinny frame had at least a hint of muscular definition in the way of delts, traps, and pecs. Bolstered by the idea that Sierra might admire my soggy, Adonis starter-kit looks, I washed my van with more cheesy poses than efficient cleaning techniques.

That's when I thought I heard someone cry out. I couldn't believe Sierra would be so bold, and besides, the voice sounded too low to be that of a teenaged girl. I lowered the garden hose, turned my head, and looked in the direction of her house. I saw nothing, but the yelling grew louder.

The water still pounding off the side of my tin-can transportation made it difficult to hear, so I dropped the hose onto the grass and turned completely toward the St. James place. Still no sign of Sierra, but the yell I heard next was unmistakable, "Over here!"

Turning my head still further to the left, I saw Ed St. James and a large animal of some sort wrestling in the dirt livestock pen behind their modest barn. "Get over here!" he yelled.

Did he know more than Sierra realized? Was he going to unleash that agitated critter on me if I got close enough? I had never had anything to do with Ed St. James, pissed off or otherwise, and this hardly seemed like a good time to get acquainted. "Get over here, goddamn it!" he barked once more.

I understood that I was under a spell that could make me do most anything his daughter suggested, but I'm not sure what compelled me to trot toward Ed. I suppose it was a mix of obeying an elder and curiosity at why he had wrestled what appeared to be a huge bull to the ground. "Hurry up!" he continued to yell.

His stock pen was outlined by three low strands of wire. The bottom two wires were barbed, but the top one was clean. Pushing it down to jump over it seemed the most expeditious means of crossing. I knew immediately that I had made a mistake. The electrical current running through the wire caused my fingers to reflexively lock around it and a strong charge rifled up my forearms and across my shoulders before it caused my modest pectoral muscles to pucker up like small lemons. "Shit!" I hissed to myself, "It's hot!"

After I worked my hands loose, I bent beneath the hot wire while I pressed down the middle strand of barbed wire and stepped between the two. "C'mon, hurry up!" he yelled again.

Ed St. James was big enough to snap me like a twig, but being repeatedly yelled at and lured into an electrically charged fence had turned me from intimidated to ticked off. If he wanted a piece of me, I was determined to give him his money's worth. But as I straightened up and resumed my trot toward the frantic farmer, the absurd scenario became clear for the first time.

The bovine he had wrestled to the ground was not a bull, but a bloated cow. Ed was sprawled in the dirt holding down her head while her foamy mouth bellowed and her rear legs twitched. "C'mon," he repeated. "I need your help!"

As I approached him, he shouted again, "Not up here, down there!" and he jerked his head toward the aft section of the distressed cow.

Slower than was acceptable to Ed St. James, I walked around toward the cow's rear end. It was swollen and encrusted with a mix of dirt, blood, and multicolored goo.

"Get down there," he shouted. "She's breech and I need you to pull the calf out!"

I just stood there, however, staring at what looked to me like an extra-large cow vagina pizza and wondered how on earth one would even consider doing what Mr. St. James had just asked me to do.

"HURRY UP, GODDAMN IT!" he screamed.

Now, thinking no more than I did when I fled the darkness of his front door just a few nights before, my bare knees ground into the dirt directly behind the struggling cow. I locked my right hand into the shape of a spear and plunged it into the hot, gooey mass before me. I pushed in what seemed to me like a very great distance. Almost up to the elbow in the cow's swollen vagina, I looked up at Ed and said, "I don't feel anything!"

"Further, damn it! Reach in further!"

I lowered my body closer to the ground, winced at the idea that my face was closer to the cow's crap-covered rectum than the gods ever intended, and pushed in even further. When I was in half-way up to my bicep I yelled, "Hey! I feel a foot!"

Ed didn't bother to correct me by saying that it was, in fact, a hoof I had latched on to. Instead he yelled, "Good! Now pull!"

I did pull, trying to ignore the ooze coating my arm as I withdrew it from the cow. After about eighteen inches, I was unable to move the hoof any further. "It's stuck." I reported.

"You gotta reach in further and find the other hoof," he said urgently.

I did as he demanded, and just as I was running out of bicep and twisting my head to avoid a bad case of manure breath, the unborn calf kicked its other hind leg into my hand. "I got it!" I yelled.

While I didn't wait for further instruction, Ed yelled anyway, "Pull, damn it! PULL!"

Just as before, the little hoof moved about eighteen inches before it slowed down, but this time it did not stop completely. I managed to rock back onto my left leg, gain a little leverage, and pull a bit harder. The old girl bellowed and I fell backward. The calf and the gooey mass that lubricated its journey suddenly sloshed from the cow and into my lap.

No one moved right away. Ed continued to hold the cow's head to make sure she didn't kick her newborn calf. Maybe my safety entered his mind, as well. But the exhausted cow was in no hurry to move. Ed stroked her neck a few times and told her she was a good old girl.

I eased myself out from under the shiny black calf and stood up, letting the afterbirth fall away from my fashionably casual attire. Soon Ed St. James was kneeling over the baby calf. I had been too overwhelmed to ascertain its condition, but Ed's gentle examination of the baby seemed to suggest it was okay.

The surreal nature of the moment reignited my inner smart-ass and I considered widening my stance, placing my hands on my hips, thrusting out my chest, and proclaiming in the deepest voice I could muster, "My work is done here."

But I didn't do that. Instead I stepped quietly backwards to begin my slow, dazed walk home. Ed must have seen my shadow move on the ground beside him, because he suddenly squinted up at me and said, "You did a fine job. Thank you."

"You're welcome," I said. At least, I think I said it.

I returned to the hose still running in our front yard and let it gush over me for a very long time. Then I retreated to the house and took an even longer shower.

As absurd as the episode had been, it left me feeling strangely contented and unusually reflective. It also left me keenly aware that the girl who had been my absolute obsession an hour before was now completely off of my radar. Yes, she was still attractive, funny, and daring, but she was no longer my conquest and I didn't really understand why.

The more I thought about it, the more it occurred to me that there was still a bit of wild in our remote corner of the Southwest. It was much wilder when my great-grandparents first ventured here many years before. Then, people lived by a code. Maybe some version of The Code of the West is what changed my feelings about pursuing Ed's daughter, Sierra.

The Code of the West no longer had much to do with horses, six-guns, or dying with your boots on, but there was still a code at play here somewhere, I was sure of it. I just needed to figure out what it was.

It took me a while, but this is what I came up with: "Once you've reached up the vagina of your neighbor's cow, you don't go messing around with his daughter."

That's a code I still live by to this day.

PARTY
AT THE GHOST TOWN

They say you can never go home again, but Mercury Elementary School had a way of proving that old adage wrong. By the beginning of my senior year, most of us could acquire all the credits we needed to graduate with only a half-day of classes. For the more studious set, this was a great opportunity to take the higher level college prep classes. For some of us, though, it meant an opportunity for school-sponsored jobs that let us pursue gainful employment and work experience in lieu of afternoon class time.

I was already well on my way to being a capable commercial artist, and with my future trade school plans pretty well considered, I knew where I was headed next fall. There were, however, no interesting artistic gigs open in Deerville. I loved sports, however, and knew the coaching assistant's job was available at my old grade school in Mercury. I liked transitioning from a morning at high school to a fun and easy job each afternoon. It was in the direction I needed to go anyway, and it wrapped up in plenty of time for me to get on to The Bull Dogger.

My senior year was off to a great start for plenty of other reasons, too. While I managed to maintain a social life, my full schedule meant I had to be fairly strategic about most every decision I made, and that had a way of keeping me out of serious trouble. That was fine with me.

Since I put a premium on quality over quantity of experience, the effort I'd put into my trusty van was paying social dividends, too. Its once utilitarian interior had been fitted with carpet, paneling, upholstery and a groovy sound system.

While my schedule made arriving at a social scene too rare to take for granted, my mobile party machine was always a welcome sight and it immediately became the center of activity. The location of each social scene, however, became an increasing challenge as the winter progressed and kids stayed out late to play on Friday nights after the home basketball games.

Cooking until 11 p.m. prevented me from attending the games, but I was happy to leave work in time to catch up with everyone afterwards. The trick was finding them. Our desert parties rotated between three "secret" locations in order to create a game of cat and mouse with the county sheriff's department. As far-flung as these locations where—two were due north of town and one was in the south—you needed to know which one was in play or it just wasn't worth the effort. This was especially true for me because I came from way east of town. I often found myself settling for just cruising Main Street or hanging out with whomever happened into the generous parking lot of one of the town's two convenience stores.

This troubling compromise got me wishing for a fourth secret party location that was more convenient to my work situation near Mercury. An eight-minute drive due south of The Bull Dogger put you in the beautiful Luna Mountain foothills, and from there I could be home in a third less time than I could from the other established locations. The ego in me even contemplated a name established in my honor, like "Greg's Gulch," but I immediately thought better of it. Why associate your name with something that would be the target of local law enforcement? No, I decided, locating a simple "Luna Gulch" would suffice.

I was thinking this challenge through early one quiet Sunday evening at the steakhouse when the idea for this fourth location slapped me like a pink porterhouse across the face. The solution did not lie in a new hunk of virgin desert but right around the corner at a top secret ghost town!

As kids, my little brother Jeff, my cousin Joey, and his neighbor and good friend, Conrad Givens, and I had ridden our bikes over every inch of earth between where they lived, adjacent to the grounds of Mercury Elementary, and where we lived, four miles to the north. Up the straight dirt road that ran for a mile and a half through the fields to the north of the school was the nasty little mud-lined Deerville canal. It paled in comparison to the larger cement-lined behemoth canal to the north. That one was fed by fresh water from the Roosevelt Irrigation District and, most importantly, fueled the watery wonderland that surrounded our house. Still, the Deerville canal was good for plunking rocks into and created a natural border for all things to its north. It was eerily quiet there. A rickety wood bridge crossed the water to absolutely nothing except a group of neglected tamarack trees. The bridge's condition was bad for trucks or tractors but was sturdy enough for curious boys exploring on bicycles.

When we found this place, we discovered one of the great treasures of our youth. Completely shrouded from view to all except the freight trains traveling on the Southern Pacific railroad track were six wood-framed structures built before the turn of the century—three modest homes, a small barn, and two little outhouses. They were oddly devoid of meaningful foundations and, as a result, leaned noticeably in one direction or another, which had caused conspicuous cracks to open at their corners. All reusable hardware had long since vanished, the windows were broken, and the screens were ripped, but for us it remained a magical place for years of secretive fun. I smiled when I remembered it and kicked myself for not taking advantage of it sooner.

My best pal, Eric Bruce, and I always did some regular pre-class cruising, and that day, I excitedly filled him in about the old ghost town. I explained that I was going to skip our ritualistic lunchtime cruising that day so I could get out to Mercury early enough to investigate the new party site's potential before my appointed time at work.

That afternoon, I gingerly eased my van across the creaky old bridge noting the disastrous barrier it could pose for a collection of reckless, half-drunk revelers. Fortunately, a subsequent survey of the area revealed an otherwise small and unnoticeable road that ran parallel to the train tracks; this would be the perfect low profile entry and exit portal. Otherwise, all was the same as I remembered.

One of the buildings looked to be just the right size. It needed a good deal of cleaning, but if we lined the perimeter with hay bales and figured out how to accommodate building a fire inside it, the place would be just right. Hay bales were cheap and plentiful nearby, but buying them was unnecessary because indefinitely "borrowing" six or seven bales was easy enough—I could abscond with them in my van if I took care not to scratch up the paneling. Then, as if to confirm this location as the perfect new party option, I found a good item to hold a fire, and that spared me the messy hunt for a discarded steel drum. The round-cornered bottom pan of an old dismantled swamp cooler was just sitting there, begging to be repurposed into a fresh new life as a "fireplace."

The next morning, a Tuesday, I shared the positive news with Eric and told him I was going to work on it this week. If I was lucky, I would have it ready for a celebration after the home basketball game that coming Friday night. Given its cool potential, however, I wanted to keep quiet about the place until I was sure everything was just right. Eric shared my enthusiasm and agreed we should keep it quiet, but then he sheepishly admitted that he couldn't help because he had an existing commitment with his longtime girlfriend, Ashley.

That was my cue to give him a bad time, but then he brightened. Ashley lived in White Sands, north of the ghost town and he would have to drive right by it to get home. This meant that at least he could come by to check it out, even if he arrived on the late side.

While I thought I was getting pretty good at staying free of real trouble by this time, when I look back on my clean-up efforts on that Wednesday afternoon, I marvel at that thought. What I was doing actually qualified as risky stupidity. On most afternoons, the coaching assistant's job was almost completely self-supervised. I knew what needed to get done and did it. At times, the job required chalking nice, straight track and field lines along the ground, but at other times, I was free to toss a ball around with a small group of my favorite kids—and I did have my favorites. There were four eighth-graders who were as funny as could be and always hung around to help with whatever I was up to. When there was nothing else to do, the boys hopped in my van and I took them to one of the school's vast, flat, and often unused playgrounds. Once there, I let them open the van's rear doors so they could ski in their socks on the slick grass as I drove in slow lazy circles away from anyone's notice.

Having that level of casual trust already established with my four favorite boys, I didn't think much about it when they offered to help with whatever I was up to that afternoon, but it was risky to sneak off campus for a couple of hours with them to get the new party digs cleaned up. Given my jammed schedule, though, it seemed that playing hooky from work was the only option available to me. All I was thinking about was that I had a big load of hay bales and all the necessary brooms and shovels in the back of my van, and that meant we all had to squeeze into the cab. It really didn't occur to me then just how crazy taking them with me was. They, of course, were thrilled just to be included on a new adventure.

There *was* an upside. We worked fast and were back at the school in just over an hour. With the bus barn's air compressor, sink, and a mountain of paper towels, we even managed to minimize the remarkable filth we covered ourselves in while converting my chosen structure from an eyesore into something worthy of a set on the TV show, *Hee Haw*.

Though it was short notice, Thursday morning Eric and I started spreading the word that I'd be leading anyone interested to a new party location around eleven-fifteen on Friday night. With the grapevine doing its thing, I made do with another abbreviated lunch so I could return to the ghost town and prep the fireplace. I was tempted to place the big pan outside the little building and hope it would throw enough light inside for everyone to appreciate the great space, but moving the pan inside was irresistible. I rearranged a couple of hay bales, elevated the pan over some big dirt clods, and positioned it near the biggest window, which was conveniently close to a gaping crack splitting up the corner of the building. It couldn't have looked better.

All Friday night at work I thought about the dozen or so people who said they were looking forward to seeing the newest spot. If most of them made it, the effort would qualify as a reasonable start, and I enjoyed work with the eager excitement that something cool was coming together for the first time in a long while.

I made it into Deerville by the appointed time, and as I approached the convenience store parking lot, it was clear that something was up. Not only was the parking lot jammed, but so were the adjacent streets. I finally managed to draw my mouth closed, realizing all these cars were awaiting the rendezvous. As appreciative as I was, I was scared that the mass of cars would attract the notice of the Deerville police department. I quickly circled the parking lot without stopping, waved my arm for all to follow, and headed back in the direction of the new party location.

Glancing back, I watched an explosion of engines and headlights burst into life. The next eight miles were too straight for me to get a clear perspective on the length of my convoy, but as I made the lone right turn onto Cotton Tail Road, I finally saw the stunning length of the illuminated ribbon behind me. It looked like some inexplicable nocturnal funeral procession racing at sixty miles per hour toward the middle of nowhere.

We more than filled the available parking space, but once all the lights died down I was satisfied that we were as invisible as I hoped we would be.

What followed couldn't have been more gratifying. People loved the new venue even before they saw it in the glow of a warm, crackling fire. As I lit it up, a chorus of ooohs and aaahs erupted from delighted kids packed into the room, sitting on the bales of hay, and standing two deep.

I was still awash in their enthusiastic approval when I heard the first cough, and then another. The blaze was burning too hard and high for my venting strategy to have the desired effect. The room's low ceiling forced the smoke down, and everyone felt it in their watering eyes and choking throats. We all waded outside, and looked in on the glowing smoke-filled room from the much colder and darker area outside. In just seconds, I'd gone from feeling uplifted to let down.

With the low, flat pan full of flames, there was no way to move it from its resting spot. It was a positive and industrious group, however, and soon flashlights emerged and people started scrounging for wood to make a fire outside the little building.

That's when Sam Yanez spoke up. "My place isn't too far from here, let's just go over there!"

Until he spoke, it was easy to forget about Sam and his weird twenty-something existence among the teens of Deerville. Sam enlisted in the Navy right out of high school and had completed his four years. He returned to Deerville and the routine he knew when he left, but he soon realized that all the people of his age had long since moved on with their lives. Sam, on the other hand, reverted to being a teen and became a quiet fixture in our social scene. That's why it seemed odd to hear him actually inviting people to the house he rented just up the road in White Sands. I guess he had a normal, paying, adult day job after all.

There were still lots of congratulatory backslaps and plenty of assurances that the ghost town was a really good spot and was going to be great. They were right, I supposed. When one fellow partier volunteered to bring the interior wash tub from an old clothes washer to serve as the outdoor fireplace at the next party, I'd already decided to buy a cheap wood burning stove to install in the party palace and get candles for illumination.

In spite of all this rationalization, I was bummed. I watched Manny Leandro do a weird fire dance of his own within the little shack, stomping out the fire in a hypnotic craze. Then, the engines started, lights came on, and the procession moved toward Sam's place.

I did not. I was at the tail end of the cars headed north, but as they continued on to the Yanez rental, I turned left onto the road to my house. It was strange—yet kind of nice—to be in bed and dozing off at such a reasonable hour on what was intended to be an eventful evening with me serving as host.

It's a good thing I turned in early, though, because I was already up when the phone rang at nine o'clock Saturday morning. It was Eric and he sounded unusually wound up. As soon as I answered, he said, "Good! You're okay?"

I was embarrassed upon hearing his voice, as I had forgotten all about his post-date promise to drop by. "I'm sorry, Eric," I answered. "I forgot all about waiting for you."

"You don't know, do you?" He hastily interrupted.

"Know what?" I asked, increasingly confused and impatient.

"It burned down last night! I was afraid you were in some kind of trouble!"

Eric went on to explain that he had made it to the ghost town at the altogether reasonable hour of one a.m. The little house was engulfed in flames and Mercury's volunteer fire department was there, fumbling about with their antique fire truck, trying to limit the damage to just the one building. He said he would have gotten closer to learn more but didn't really want to attract the notice of the sheriff's officers who seemed to really be enjoying the show.

I assume Manny's attempt at stomping out the fire must have sent cinders flying in all directions. The bone dry wood floors wouldn't take long to erupt in flames.

I spent another long day at the house Saturday and at work that night fearing that one of those sheriffs might show up to ask questions about the suspicious fire—or even outright arson—the night before. Fortunately, no such inquiries emerged over the long, worrisome weekend and I was able to return to school on Monday to simply deal with the response of my fellow students.

It was a strange, mixed bag of reactions. In the wake of the fire, I couldn't help but feel the whole effort was an embarrassing flub, but the overall reception I received around Deerville High had the vibe of "How cool was that?!"

Upon arriving at Mercury Elementary that afternoon, I hardly noticed when Mrs. Denning, Uncle CT's secretary, summoned me to the office over the school's loud speaker system.

I knew Wilma Denning much better than simply as the person who helped my uncle run the little school because she played piano at the church I attended since I was a small boy. More importantly, Wilma was the mom of my friend Ozzie Denning, and I knew he inherited his wicked sense of humor directly from her.

As I sat quietly before her, she asked coyly, "Do anything exciting this weekend?"

"Shit!" I thought to myself. "She knew! Ozzie must have been her source."

Choosing my words carefully, I said, "Noooo, pretty quiet for me, but I did hear the volunteer fire department had a fun workout."

"Oh, yes," she responded. "You know my oldest son is on the crew and had a great time. They even got to try sucking water into their pump motor from the Deerville canal!"

I simply nodded and tried to maintain an appropriate, respectable smile.

She finally broke the silence again. "Well, I'm glad you're fine and I just wanted to remind you how important it is to be careful out there. You know, you never want to arm too many people with information that could prove difficult for you." And then she concluded with a barely perceptible wink.

She was right, of course. While the events of the previous weekend were common knowledge to many, connecting the dots had thus far escaped the notice of the police.

"Thank you," I said. "And if there is ever anything I can do for you—" While I doubted she would ever call in the favor, offering one seemed the least I could do for this chronically cool lady.

Years later, I noticed the area around the little old ghost town had been cleared and decked out with a unique multi-dimensional house and a landscape that stood out compared to most other rural construction efforts. If the ghost town had to go, I was glad it gave way to such a handsome and creative homestead.

And, on some level, I took just a little credit for getting some of the old out of the way for the new.

THE MILK TRUCK HAS LANDED

One truism of life in the desert was the absolute, indisputable need for private transportation. And in an environment where the distance between my home and those of my friends was measured in miles rather than blocks, my appreciation for the wheel developed at a very early age.

Enter the bicycle. It allowed me to meet friends at the grade school for a game of football, ride to the canal for a swim, or even pedal to Robbie Jamison's tamarack trees for the quarterly BB gun war. Once, I shot Robbie in the gut, and he never forgave me because he claimed to have surrendered. Sure, his hands were clasped behind his head, but I argued that he may have had a dagger concealed in his collar. So what if he wasn't wearing a shirt?

We boys also knew we could use our bikes for purposes other than recreation. There were always the income-building pursuits of lawn mowing or cleaning chalk boards after school. With any luck, we all hoped we could save enough by our sixteenth birthdays for that all important upgrade in transportation—our first piece-of-crap cars.

A car was what separated the guys from the boys. Mine was the first generation to get hammered with the campaign, "To get a good job, you have to have a good education." Naturally, we debated the validity of that message. Everyone agreed, however, that to get a date, you had to at least have a piece-of-crap car.

I was hooked on cars the way some kids were hooked on drugs. It was the same vicious cycle. Better transportation meant better income opportunities. Better income meant better transportation. Before I knew what was happening, I had moved up to the hard stuff, a new El Camino Super Sport. It was beautiful, fast, and reliable. But beyond that, it was boring.

Gone was the cheap thrill of simply making it to school without breaking down in front of those stinking stockyards. My fingernails were suddenly free of grime and my knuckles healed up nicely, but I missed the challenge of struggling against a grease-laden engine. There were other consequences of having a nice car, as well. Friends noticed my swearing lost the rhythm and creativity that was its hallmark during those days when my life was more mechanically challenged. I had a bad case of clunker withdrawal.

I found my fix sitting next to an isolated, rundown, wooden-framed house. It was way out where the canal slowed to a trickle and created a crystal clear, but leech-infested, pool. I had just learned the hard way that still waters not only run deep, but they can also leave you looking like Humphrey Bogart in *The African Queen*. That day, those "nasty buggers" brought an abrupt end to an impromptu swim with my girlfriend, Lisa. We had just finished coaxing the slippery, liver-like parasites from our nether regions when I looked up and saw it. It was big, boxy, and generally homely, but it made my pulse race all the same. As I stood there shaking, I knew I had to have it. Ten minutes and $125 dollars later, I was the proud owner of a 1952 Divco milk truck. The leeches were suddenly worth the trouble.

It was a remarkable machine. Its center-hinged hood sloped to a substantial grill flanked by torpedo-coned head lamps. Comically bulbous fenders shrouded tall, twenty-inch tires at the front of the truck, while a serious set of dual-rimmed wheels anchored a one-ton suspension at its rear.

There were three options for revving its Continental, flat-head, six-cylinder engine. First, it featured a conventional gas pedal. Second, there was a foot feed in the floor pan for stand-up driving when the swing-away driver's seat was disengaged. Finally, there was a hand feed on the T-handled gear shift lever mounted to the steering column. The cab could be entered from either side through school bus style doors. The rear doors to the cargo area could be locked open in wide and extra-wide configurations.

The stubby, oxidized blue milk truck was all I could have hoped for in a second vehicle. It was stupid, frivolous fun. I put the ancient workhorse back in the business of hauling heavy loads. This time, however, the cargo was human rather than dairy.

Sunset drives often featured the milk truck winding along the canal bank with its cargo doors locked open. It kicked up bellows of rolling dust while my crew of assorted cousins in the back belted out Santana's campfire classic, "Oye Como Va."

On moonlit nights, the milk truck was pressed into public service, perhaps to liven up a desert party. Although attended by dozens of drunken adolescents, these were strangely sober affairs. Most the fun stemmed from watching a party-goer attempt to make his or her "bladder flatter." This required staggering into the darkness beyond the flickering light of the bonfire. A sudden explosion of profanity always meant the thoroughly hydrated reveler had run afoul of a cactus.

The milk truck could accommodate eight comfortably or eighteen *very* comfortably. Perhaps the best thing about it was that it offered the post-pubescent equivalent of a pony ride. Bouncing a coed collection of teenagers through mesquite trees and across dry river beds afforded a degree of consensual contact without the effort or expense of an actual date.

Perhaps a spin in the milk truck also generated excitement because it only happened on rare occasions. You see, putting the vintage tin on the road required a bit of planning.

It was a wonderfully reliable machine once it was on the road, but its defective starter made getting it there an ordeal. You needed a fairly hefty vehicle to push or pull the milk truck into action. Once it was running, turning it on and off wasn't an option, so every trip had to begin with a completely full tank of gas.

One evening, Eric Bruce and I saw to those details plus the added precautionary measure of icing down a case of beer. We knew better than to travel in the desert without plenty of fluids on hand. Then it was time to pick up our girlfriends, Lisa and Ashley, for a twilight drive into the desert.

We each had plenty of asinine stunts to our individual credit, but when Eric and I were together, our stupidity was truly inspired. I don't know if it was fate or folly, but on this particular evening, we found ourselves approaching "the hill."

"The hill" was one of many foothills adjacent to the White Sands mountain range. What made this particular hill irresistible to gear heads was a north face just slightly too step to ascend. The pattern of attempts was pretty routine. Soon after some farmer got a new pickup truck, his kid started bragging about how unbelievable it was, throwing the word "bitchen" around way too loosely. The next thing you knew, someone challenged him to try the hill. The kid always tried in vain to drive up the hill, beating the hell out of the new pickup in the process. In turn, of course, the farmer always beat the hell out of his kid. Every once in a while, however, the perfect blend of intoxication and machinery resulted in a successful ascent. The diehard driver who conquered the hill was rewarded with a small mesa at the summit. This spot was perfect for the driver's obligatory victory dance, which often included a celebratory pee down the dusty slope he just conquered.

On this warm summer evening, the hill was unoccupied and while we hadn't discussed it, let alone planned it, we suddenly found ourselves driving up its base. At first we laughed. The idea of taking an antiquated delivery truck up a grade that humbled new four-wheel drive vehicles seemed preposterous, but we knew our buddies would be delighted to learn of our absurd effort, so we pressed on. Our laughter turned into game-face determination as the milk truck lumbered over the rocks and through the softened dirt that sent newer, lighter trucks spinning in failure off either side of the hill. Lisa managed a nervous smile of support. Ashley didn't bother. Still in first gear, I mashed the accelerator to the floor and the milk truck groaned over the crest of the hill.

Safely atop the summit, Eric and I instinctively sprang from the cab and engaged in our own bizarre victory dance. Only the presence of our girlfriends prevented us from spontaneously urinating off the edge of the hill onto the dusty course we just conquered. No wonder the first man on the moon stumbled over his line about "one small step." He was probably consumed with thoughts of whipping it out and spelling N-E-A-L.

Moments later, we toasted the climb from the cot mattresses that passed for upholstery in the back of the milk truck. Eric suggested we rotate the truck so its open cargo area faced directly west to allow a better view of the setting sun. I didn't much care, neither did Lisa or Ashley, but Eric insisted. I motioned him toward the cab of the perpetually running milk truck.

We tried to stay out of the way as Eric coaxed the vehicle forward a few feet, cranking its huge steering wheel as far as he could before backing up again. On his third such effort, the grim reaper of bad karma reached down and slapped Eric across the head for one of his countless past indiscretions. I don't know if Eric dumped the clutch too quickly, didn't give it enough gas, or both. What I do know is that he somehow managed to stall the engine.

The next few moments were remarkably quiet. I stood there pondering the big blue milk truck. It sat idle atop a small desert mountain at least fifteen miles from what could only loosely be described as civilization. The silence was shattered as I unleashed a string of profanities that would have made a construction worker blush. Eric interrupted my tirade by shouting, "I've got it! I've got it! Let's push it off the edge and I'll start it as it rolls down!"

Even by Eric's standard, this was an incredibly stupid idea. "You're crazy," I said, "you'll die for sure."

Lisa and Ashley must have been suspicious of our motives and the validity of our mechanical dilemma. "We'll help push," they volunteered.

My judgment still clouded by frustration, I directed our dates on each side of me, and with a series of short primal grunts, we eased the milk truck, with Eric sitting white-knuckled at the wheel, over the edge of the hill.

I was immediately struck with the insanity of what we had just done. Unlike the scarred portion of the hill we ascended, the side Eric looked down with roller coaster terror was much steeper and adorned with features common to the raw, foreboding desert.

The milk truck didn't so much roll as free-fall for the first thirty yards before it crashed onto the rocky surface. As a variety of desert wildlife scattered for new cover, I envisioned the milk truck bursting into a rolling ball of fire. I wondered how would I explain to Mrs. Bruce that I had turned her son into Eric Flambé? But the milk truck didn't explode. It bounced high in the air and twisted slightly to the left, then smashed to the ground again just in time to mow down a fledgling Palo Verde tree. The milk truck bounced skyward once more and twisted the other direction as it rattled through a gauntlet of assorted boulders.

I glanced at the girls—they were frozen in fear. Then I looked back down the hill at the pitiful site. The milk truck was rolling very slowly, its meandering course determined entirely by the landscape. It was obvious that Eric was out of commission.

When the milk truck was nearly at a standstill, I heard a faint noise, "Blub." Eric wasn't out of commission. He was trying to start the engine!

Lisa, Ashley, and I instinctively clasped hands and stood motionless to listen closer, "Blub, blub, blub." We began to hop up and down like Jimmy Stewart's weathered ground crew when he attempted to fire up the make-shift aircraft in *The Flight of the Phoenix*. "Blub, blub, blub, blub, blub, blub, blub, blub."

After Eric navigated the milk truck back up the hill for our hysterically joyous reunion, he explained how he was thrown from the driver's seat during the free-fall. He bounced around like a pinball for the balance of the ride. Eric credited the dingy "mattresses o' love" with preventing him from being knocked unconscious. He regained his bearings just before the milk truck came to a stop. Without time to get his butt in the driver's seat, much less his foot on the clutch, Eric lunged for the gear shift lever. He was able to grind it into second gear and twist the hand feed accelerator lever just in time for the engine to fire.

A few weeks later, I was watching news footage of a helicopter rescuing an over-zealous, under-skilled climber from Arizona's popular Squaw Peak mountain preserve. It reminded me that if Eric wasn't certifiably crazy, there would have been similar video tape of my big blue milk truck sitting high on the hill. I supposed it would have looked like one of those artist's conceptions of Noah's Arc nestled in a mountain range somewhere in the Middle East.

It would have almost been worth it. Not quite, but almost.

A HAIRY DILEMMA

Most everything in last half of my senior year improved as a result of lucky timing. I was generally sincere about college aspirations but also well aware that I didn't need a degree to enter my chosen field of work. As a budding commercial artist, I was already picking up valuable freelance work and had a possibility of near-term employment.

Even the social implications of Arizona's politically controversial decision to drop the legal drinking age to nineteen were working in my favor. Beer, the nectar of the lesser Gods, was a must to me and most every other high school kid's social life, and getting it was as frustrating as it was funny.

At seventeen, I was on the young side of my class. Many of my friends were already eighteen and ever closer to the legal drinking age. They tried a number of tricks I never bothered with, such as fake IDs or simply hoping not to get carded by busy convenience store workers. The problem in our small town was that these same clerks had been selling us Dr. Pepper and Twinkies since we received our driver's licenses. They knew our high school status from the daytime schedules we kept and had a pretty good idea that we were not yet old enough to legally buy alcohol. Some kids tried to get lucky at less familiar bars, liquor stores, or even grocery stores, but that rarely succeeded, and it was embarrassing when it failed.

This pent-up demand produced another unsightly phenomenon that I was determined to avoid—wimpy, ill-advised attempts at growing facial hair. For everyone one kid who could produce a respectable mustache before the age of nineteen, there were nine others with thin, wispy hairs struggling to conceal vast open spaces on their upper lips.

As a result of all this, what developed was a small network of enablers who were old enough to legally buy booze for us. This worked out, but it left a great deal to be desired. For starters, their 25% commission, meaning they kept one six-pack out of every case of four, was expensive. Adding to the inefficiency was the wait for one of them to happen by. Given the demands of school and my two-job schedule, I wasn't one to just sit and wait.

Early one Saturday morning, I drove alone for ninety-minutes to the east, past Phoenix, and into the snootiness of the elegant business section of Scottsdale. I entered an establishment whose Yellow Page ad stated they dealt in discreet hair solutions for men. It was clearly a high-end rug shop, but the toupee atop the head of the portly and unfailingly polite salesman who assisted me was a darned good one. I found myself really enjoying the fun and he never once made me feel like the goofy, presumptuous kid I obviously was.

For the next forty minutes, we sat before his mirror as he produced a variety of fine men's natural hair mustache options. We finally settled on one that perfectly complemented my face and hair color. I emerged with what looked like a long caterpillar in a clear protective case and the requisite spirit gum adhesive and cleaner. At the time, I didn't realize that my beautifully simple solution to the beer acquisition problem would have such a delightfully silly effect on me and my friends for the balance of the school year. It remains to this day the best $14.75 investment I ever made.

A day later Eric and I were in the parking lot of a convenience store and he couldn't believe how the intricate mesh that affixed the hairpiece to my lip allowed me to talk and even laugh without concern. We walked into the store and it was as though I had transformed into someone completely unknown to a clerk who had otherwise seen me many times. This time, however, he rang up my six-pack of Coors and big bag of barbeque potato chips as if my dad were buying them.

It worked like a charm each and every time. So much so, in fact, that I finally had to make clear that I wasn't in the business of buying booze for the masses. I did, however, always take great care of my little gang of fascinated friends. For easily buying liquor, the mustache more than achieved its purpose; we were like *made men*, no longer at the mercy of the cumbersome routine that preceded my mustache acquisition. I was only too happy to refer others to my refined hair hustling friend in Scottsdale, but to my knowledge, no one else ever bothered to make such an investment.

As spring wore on and graduation approached, the novelty of my trustworthy mustache began to wear off and I simply enjoyed it for its intended purpose. For others, it was in demand, so I agreed to share it with a few close friends, holding them to promises of no nastiness. I always cleaned it carefully upon its return. That last rule didn't really apply to Eric when he borrowed it for a night out with his gorgeous girlfriend Ashley. He could have dusted her cookies with it and I would have been reluctant to clean it for a while.

When photographs were taken for the "most" section of the yearbook, Eric thought it would be funny to wear the mustache for his "most handsome" boy picture. I agreed and was happy to loan it to him, but even I was impressed at the level to which he outdid himself. He also shaved off his envied head of always perfect hair and sported an intimidating pair of dark glasses. It looked to the unenlightened as though our most handsome boy was actually a menacing street thug who had threatened others into selecting him.

I guess in terms of being threatening, I shouldn't talk, because it reminds me of my last crazy hurrah with the trusty hair piece. It was the summer after graduation, and Eric and I had piled into his Ford pickup with our dates and gone all the way to west Phoenix for an early, heat-beating movie. On the way home, we hit the last available pizza parlor expecting a quiet dinner of cheesy pie and cold beer. We didn't expect to get carded, but I glued on the mustache as a precaution.

Our modest expectations should have been lower. The bitter, flabby manager of the restaurant made his appearance when Ashley, a year older than Eric at nineteen and of legal age, attempted to order a pitcher of beer. Ironically, the curt manager was only a year or two older than the pretty girl who stood patiently before him. He wore a tragically thin mustache of his own while I looked on politely from behind my impressive facial façade and tried not to think about how poorly endowed he must have been. Something had to be at the root of his inherent surliness and it couldn't have been us. We had just arrived and were still on our best behavior.

He studied her authentic driver's license suspiciously before he declared that Ashley and I could drink, but that Eric, who couldn't produce an ID when asked, and my date, a winsome-looking sixteen-year-old, could not. Eric was still recovering from having shorn his locks and sported a short buzz seen only on military types and those crazy enough to shave their heads for yearbook photos. We conceded that my date, Emma, was underage and we'd take a pitcher of Coke for her, but we offered that Eric was on leave from the service and embarrassed that he didn't have his ID handy. "But surely, he would be allowed to drink?" Ashley asked calmly and with a pleasant smile.

"Like I said," the manager interrupted abruptly, "you and the guy can drink, but Army boy and the girl stick to Coke. And I will be watching you."

Embarrassed glances from the staff of pizza workers seemed to confirm the manager's small weenie status. But with options so limited, we reluctantly paid and found a table that made the manager's promise to watch us as difficult as possible.

It didn't help that the pizza was lame and that the manager made good on his promise keep us under surveillance. He must have been burned for serving someone underage in the past, because the way he stalked past us bordered on intrusive and really put me my off my beer. Even worse, it got my young brain thinking of ways to conclude the evening with an appropriate gesture, some non-verbal way of clearly expressing, "Thank you, and screw you very, very much."

As it turned out, the snotty young manager made no effort to thank us for our business as we began to leave. This gave me the opportunity to complement my efforts with a little polite talk. I stopped before him, nodded, smiled faintly, and said, "Thanks. Honestly, the pizza could have been better, but the beer was nice and cold and I really enjoyed it." And with that, I calmly took the right corner of the mustache and slowly peeled it from my upper lip. His eyes grew as big as the oversize pizza pans clanking about behind him.

Whatever Steve McQueen subtlety I could maintain in my faint smile became more difficult as Eric howled with laughter on his walk toward the front door. Ashley's attempts at suppressing her guffaws failed as well, while my younger, jittery date just hurried to join them and get out the front door safely. Even the manager's long-suffering crew failed to conceal their collective snickering.

Bringing up the up rear, I smiled more fully now, turned away from the reddening young pizza boss and casually walked out the door. Seconds later, we were again seated in Eric's pickup as he prepared to back away. That's when the pissed off manager made the mistake of wildly swinging open the front door to follow us out. I suspect he simply wanted to defiantly fold his arms across his chest to better glare at us as we drove away, but we'll never know for sure because I suddenly bolted from the cab of the pickup and rushed toward him.

Without thinking, I transformed into that wild-eyed little kid who had suddenly had enough of his big brother's abuse. These rare occasions resulted in the unnatural sight of a small human being wildly chasing a much larger one around the house.

The horrified manager screamed louder than Janet Lee in *Psycho*, spun back inside the big wood and glass door and managed to lock it just before I lunged toward its handle. Through the glass, I watched the color drain from his shocked expression as he backed away from my frantic rattling of the door. That's when I heard Eric call out, "GREG, WE'D BETTER BE GOING NOW!"

With the arrival of fall, I turned nineteen and no longer needed my trusty mustache, but something interesting happened the following spring. I was working as a graphic designer with the NBC affiliate in Phoenix when a swinging thirty-something staffer insisted that the guys engage in a beard growing contest. It was, after all, the mid-seventies with all the flare pants, big shoes, and facial hair that the disco era demanded. The poor initiator of the contest endured considerable abuse for the thin, wispy growth that crept ever so slowly across his face, but my beard and moustache filled in quite nicely.

I didn't care about the outcome of the contest, but as the kid who was years younger than many of my co-workers, it was nice to suddenly have the appearance of someone older. So, I kept the beard. In fact, I kept it until I was thirty-seven.

Now that's good value.

POMP AND CIRCUMSTANTIAL EVIDENCE

With high school graduation just weeks away, I colluded with my best pal, Eric Bruce, on a truly significant send-off. I hoped for a soiree worthy of all the silliness we had endured together, and our crude but comfortable family cabin in the coolest pines of Arizona's brilliant rim country seemed the obvious setting.

Given the long hours I worked, coupled with the fact that I hadn't been caught doing anything embarrassing in a while, my parents rewarded me with their approval. So, with much excitement, Eric and I set about comprising the perfect short list of invitees.

The obvious first choice was our mutual best pal and partner in crime, Harlan Davids. For me, all that really mattered was having the three of us together. Anyone else would be gravy, but that stated, the rest of the group was pretty fun as well.

First on the list was Gabe Ramirez—a tough but gentle, wise-cracking nice guy rolled into one contradictory package.

Next was Fat Juan Rubios. His full cheeks and perpetual smile reduced his dark eyes to mere slits, but they missed nothing and his restrained insights were always funny. Once, I found Fat Juan and Harlan in Harlan's pickup at a convenience store parking lot eating just-fashioned baloney roll-ups on squishy white bread. They were sitting in absolute silence. I wandered up to Harlan's window and asked, "What are you guys doing?"

With a straight face, Harlan deadpanned, "Nothing…just listening to Bread." Bread was a syrupy sweet pop group of the early 70's. I looked down at the eight-track player hanging beneath the dash and saw that it was overflowing with the soft sandwich slices.

When I stopped laughing I asked, "Geez, how long have you been waiting here for someone to come up and ask you this?"

"Too long, man," came Harlan's reply. He and Fat Juan laughed wildly. "We're sure glad you showed up!"

Even quieter than Juan was the last of our dirty half-dozen, Griffin Bradley. The gentle giant was six feet, four inches of toothy grins, fair skin, freckles, and wavy red hair.

With the team locked, we split up assignments to gather everything from food to firearms, fishing gear to booze.

Then, only days prior to graduation night, everything changed. Eric dropped out. He and his girlfriend, Ashley, had been dating for two years and he was practically a member of her family. As such, he caved in to the pressure to be a part of their family plans rather than participate in what was starting to look like four days and three nights of completely unsupervised nonsense with the boys. Yes, of course, he was completely pussy whipped, but if you could have seen how gorgeous Ashley was you would almost understand.

While everyone felt a little let down, I was *really* bummed out. My demanding work schedule meant the cruising Eric and I did before school and during lunch made us closer friends than I was with the other guys. Plus, for the past two years, he and Ashley had been double-date constants regardless of who I was going out with.

The rest of the guys were still so enthusiastic, though, that I had no choice but to conceal my disappointment. Without Eric, I suddenly felt more like a host than a participant, but I had to set that aside to deal with another, more pressing issue. How were we going to replace Eric in our driving scheme, which anticipated two guys each in of the three pickups we needed to haul all of our gear up to the cabin? Hoping to avoid a broad group of acquaintances competing for Eric's open spot, we quickly and quietly chose Perry Thompson to ride up with us. Diminutive and smart, Perry was a rich farmer kid who graduated the year prior. He had been out of town attending agriculture classes at Arizona State and was thrilled at the chance to reconnect. We were friends but never had the opportunity to hang out much, so I invited him to ride with me.

Graduation went off without a hitch on Tuesday night and we all kept our celebrations well under control knowing we'd set off early Wednesday for the *real* celebration.

Since it was very early June, we were on the road and in the pines before the summer-long visitors arrived, and it was mid-week to boot. The freedom of the near-empty mountain road was intoxicating, and intoxication was a big part of the agenda. Once we arrived, everyone was duly impressed with the cabin, especially its solitude.

We drank, fished out of my Dad's rowboat in the nearest lake, drank, barbecued, drank, and told lies around a campfire before drinking some more and finally going to bed.

I contemplated our busy first day while I flipped pancakes on the griddle in the middle of my mom's vintage gas stove the following morning. Since we had done so much the day before, I was glad we were getting off to a slower start the second day.

The respite was short-lived. Not long after breakfast, the six of us went strolling through the forest past some unoccupied cabins toward the dump. While that sounds sordid, the dump was such a beauty that its name needed updating. Dumping duties had actually been turned over to a commercial trash crusher that wasn't anywhere near the old, thoroughly cleaned up landfill. The change had left a huge, wide open meadow dotted with pretty bodies of water.

By that morning, we were already used to having the forest to ourselves and it showed in our appearance. We wore a bizarre combination of hats, bathrobes, boxer shorts, and cowboy boots. Everyone was armed with a rifle in one hand and a six-pack in the other, the latter providing not only refreshment but aluminum for cans for target practice. Hunter S. Thompson would have approved.

Having just shot the hell out of anything that could loosely be described as a target, everyone seemed content to simply shoot the breeze on the walk back to the cabin. As others talked and joked, the host in me couldn't help but wonder about what was next. It had been good fun so far, but from fishing to bullshitting around the firepit, whatever we did next would qualify as a repeat. That's when Fat Juan Rubios bailed me out.

"I know I'm one of only two genuine Mexicans on this trip, but is anyone else hurting for some beef enchiladas?" he asked.

The group responded positively and Harlan quickly asked, "How about it, Greg?"

Just like that, we had something new to do. "Payson is lovely this time of year," I responded.

A few hours later, we were all cleaned up and winding down the mountain road toward Payson. The lovely old town was home to high country cowboys, happy retirees, and one the state's better rodeos. Most importantly, it was also home to some darn good Mexican food and I had a place in mind. It would not have mattered, however, if I didn't have a favorite spot because we would have found something. It seems a town couldn't survive in Arizona without a variety of good Mexican food joints.

Once again our inefficient convoy of six guys seated two abreast in three two-seater pickups took to the road. I lead the way down the rim in my El Camino. Gabe followed me in his short bed Chevy pickup. Bringing up the rear was Fat Juan's long bed Ford work truck. It was the one that dutifully hauled my Dad's rowboat up to the cabin.

Halfway to Payson I looked up into my rearview mirror and saw that Gabe had pulled his truck over to the side of the road. Fat Juan pulled in behind him as I hit my brakes, then backed up and joined them. Gabe had gotten a flat. That was fine because we had nothing but time and it was good to just lean on our vehicles, laugh, and enjoy the outdoors while Gabe changed his tire.

Once in Payson, I led them to my favorite gas station. It was an ancient, family-owned independent that sported a rustic little repair bay, a small general store, and an entryway that was flanked by a big plaster elk on one side and an even more impressive, six-foot plus, hand-carved, wooden Indian on the other. The attendant told Gabe he could fix the tire but the wait could be a half hour or more. "No problem," I said, and I pointed to a bar I referred to as a pool hall a few blocks up Main Street. "Can you just call us there when it's done?" I asked.

"Happy to," said the young attendant, "I know their number by heart."

And with that, we took off.

Afternoon was easing into twilight as we entered the vintage bar. I was just seventeen, most of the others were eighteen, but Arizona had lowered its drinking age to nineteen two years prior and Perry could legally order a couple of pitchers of beer. The barkeep didn't bother to card the rest of us. I must admit, we were so enjoying the moment and knocking our two-man teams on and off the pool table that I was sorry when the phone finally rang. Fat Juan and Gabe left to pick up the fixed flat tire. The rest of us stayed and continued to shoot pool. By the time they returned, I figured, we all would be eager to eat.

But after a couple of minutes, the phone rang again and the nonplussed barkeep called out, "Greg!" Getting a call at the little saloon surprised me, but it was nothing compared to the surprise I felt when I got on the phone.

On the other end of the line, Gabe deadpanned, "I'm trying to get out of town." This was part of the challenge when talking with Gabe, he deadpanned everything and joked around a lot—a problem made more difficult since the phone prevented me from seeing his face.

In spite of my concern, I fought the urge to take the bait. "Sounds dramatic," I answered back.

"No, really," Gabe continued, "Juan and I paid for the tire and then kind of threw that wooden Indian in the back of my truck before we left, but I think the kid at the gas station called the cops."

"Oh shit," I responded. "You think you can find your way back to the cabin?"

"No," he replied, "but I can get to the turn-off to the cabins."

"That's good," I said. "Dump that thing anywhere you can and we'll meet back up the hill." We quickly settled our tab, exited the bar, and climbed back into our vehicles.

It was growing dark as we pulled out onto the street and we kept our eyes peeled for Gabe and Juan. There was no sign of them, but I was relieved that there were no racing patrol cars or flashing lights to be seen either. Maybe the guys had made it safely off Main Street and into the woods.

My optimism faded when we got back up the hill and slowed for the cabin turn-off from the main road. This is the spot was Gabe was supposed to meet us, but a slow cruise around the shadowy hiding spots revealed nothing. Since there was no point in proceeding into the maze of dirt roads dotted by similar-looking cabins, we dropped the tailgate on my El Camino, took a seat, cracked open a few beers, and waited.

After a good stretch of time the guys still had not arrived and I suggested, "No point in driving all the way back to Payson, we'd never find them."

"No," Harlan interjected, "'cause they're probably already in jail."

Ever positive, Griffin countered with, "You don't know, if they got off the road and killed their lights they might just sit in the dark until morning."

"Maybe," Harlan chuckled, "but I doubt it, 'cause they're probably already in jail."

We waited there a bit longer until Perry finally complained, "My butt hurts." And with that, I led us back to my parent's cabin.

With no phone service to the cabins, there was no way for them to call and enlighten us.

Fearing the worst, we packed up and got back to the turn-off from the main road bright and early the next morning. We still hoped for the best—a reunion with our missing comrades who would fill in the details of the previous night's adventure. But unfortunately, they still were not waiting for us at the agreed-upon spot.

There was a trailer space rental facility near the main road turn-off and it had a pay phone. Armed with a handful of change, Perry called the Payson police department.

The officer who answered gleefully acknowledged their apprehension of two thieves fitting the description of our friends. Never mind that Perry had already given the officer on the phone our friend's names. Clearly, the small town police were still feeling pumped up in the wake of the crime spree Gabe and Juan unleashed on Payson the night before.

The cop on the phone said, "It would be real helpful if you boys could stop by and relieve us of a pickup belonging to one Mr. Ramirez." Since hope springs eternal, "helpful" was what we wanted to be. Before we continued, we all handed Perry our cash in the hope that our smooth-talking friend could work something out that would allow us to leave the police station with our sextet intact.

After we got there, we learned that Gabe had made it far enough off of Main Street to escape our sight, but not that of the patrolman who pulled him over in short order.

Still later, after Gabe's release, he gave us additional details. It seems that after the behemoth Payson patrolman removed his flashlight's glare from Gabe's squinting eyes, he pointed it into the bed of his pickup and ran it up and down the massive carved Indian. He then returned the beam to Gabe's face and asked, "Where'd you get the Indian?"

I could well imagine the subdued mock surprise with which Gabe responded, "What Indian?" We figured that was probably the shortest interrogation in Payson police history.

Things weren't going any better as we waited in the police station for Perry to work his magic. The Payson police didn't care much for valley kids, rural or otherwise, coming up north to cause trouble and steal their landmarks. It didn't help any that Gabe, upon hearing our presence in the lobby, was acting up again. He rattled the bars of his cell and screeched out a shockingly good impersonation of the world-famous chimpanzee "Cheetah." I'm sure Fat Juan was seated not far away, taking it all in through those laughing, dark eyes.

The policeman explained there was no bail to be worked out. That would happen at an arraignment scheduled for a few days later, but the monkeys—err, boys rather—would be well cared for until then.

We returned to the parking lot to find two large policemen struggling to remove the huge, heavy carving from the back of the pickup. I'm sure they were more concerned with protecting the Indian's carefully applied paint than that of Gabe's pickup bed. Giant Griffin along with Harlan, who was pretty hefty himself, huffed and puffed in assistance. I had to smile at the sight. It was a reminder of what an adrenalin rush can come from a sudden, irresistible opportunity to be ornery. Let's remember that this obviously weighty artwork had, just a few hours earlier, been deftly lifted by just two excited young guys.

Once they completed that chore, Harlan slipped behind the wheel of Gabe's pickup and our conspicuously under-populated convoy returned to Main Street and eased its way out of town. Once we were safely beyond its borders and onto the first empty stretch of long and relatively straight road, Harlan eased over to the shoulder and stopped while Griffin, piloting Fat Juan's work truck, then Perry and I in my El Camino, pulled in behind.

Harlan strolled past me to an ice chest in the bed of my car. He removed three six-packs and, with his trademark sly grin, handed me one of them and asked, "This is kind of a long drive, right?" He handed another one through the window to Griffin without breaking his stride, and returned to Gabe's pickup, keeping the last one for himself.

I was in the rear but ready to go, and I doubted that anyone would begrudge my El Camino its rightful place at the front of our trio. So, without delay, I roared past Harlan with a completely unnecessary high-velocity roar. I couldn't help but notice him flash his charming smile.

Within a few short moments, he had pulled the front bumper of Gabe's pickup to with a few feet of my rear one—and that could mean only one thing. We were going to race. This fact was confirmed by the easy smile gazing back at me through my rearview mirror. "Did you buckle up?" I asked Perry. He didn't answer, but I couldn't miss the clearly audible "click" of his seat belt. And with that, I laid on the accelerator and easily pulled away from Harlan.

At that point, it was great fun and still relatively safe because the road was fairly forgiving, but that would change soon—we were approaching an endless series of winding turns with only occasional straightaways.

Before I could reduce my speed, Harlan restored himself to a few short car lengths behind me. "Holy cow," I said to Perry. "What's Gabe got in that thing?" Even if it could boast a bigger engine, I should have had no problem putting distance between myself and Harlan. My El Camino was essentially a car with a pitiful little pickup bed where there would normally be a more practical back seat and trunk. Plus, my car had all the high performance options to support its "Super Sport" badging. Yet there was Harlan, right on top of me, smiling that trademark smile.

Perry never did respond. It seemed he had become one with the upholstery, and I couldn't blame him. We went well over a hundred miles per hour on anything remotely straight, and I maintained as much speed as I could on the relentless curves, usually staying in the high sixties to eighties.

The episode reminded me that, in his own way, Harlan was just as crazy as Gabe. I had the option to ease off the accelerator. I could have relaxed my white-knuckled grip on the steering wheel, let Harlan pass me and bring this silliness to an end. That would have been especially nice for poor Perry for whom I was feeling some genuine sympathy, but of course, I could not do that because it would bring all this machismo fun to a wimpy end. But at least I knew enough to be genuinely scared. I caught a glimpse in my rearview mirror of the always relaxed Harlan, driving at triple-digit speeds with just his non-dominant left wrist casually draped over the top of the steering wheel, while cocking his head back for a mouthful of beer from the can in his right. It was amazing and horrifying all at once.

Finally, mercifully, the hilly twists gave way to longer stretches of straight road as we emerged from the hills toward the much hotter, flatter, wider, and more populated confines of the desert valley. In the recreational area where the Gila and Salt rivers come together, I hit my right turn indicator, eased carefully off the gas, and slowed to a stop on the side of a generous pull-out. Harlan followed suit.

He got out of Gabe's pickup, grinned, stretched, lowered the tailgate, and casually took a seat before gently swinging his feet. Perry walked gingerly over and rested his chin on his forearms, happy, no doubt, that his still shaking five-foot, six-inch frame was largely concealed by the high bed sides. I joined Harlan on the tailgate, trying to look casual about a road race I was truly glad to have behind us and glanced at my wristwatch. "Holy shit!" I exclaimed as Harlan looked easily my way and waited for me to elaborate.

"People usually allow about two hours for that stretch of road given that you do most of it in the forties and fifties. By my watch, we left Payson just forty-two minutes ago."

We were having a good chuckle at that when we were interrupted by the unmistakable "pop-pop-pop" of Griffin quickly pulling his foot of the gas of Fat Juan's lumbering work truck. We had lost sight of him miles ago and were understandably expecting a long wait. Seems he too had made remarkably good time. Hardly ever demonstrative, even Harlan muttered an admiring "Dammmmn."

Given that our trip featured several of the most reckless partiers of our class, there were plenty of people waiting for full reports. I wondered if news of the arrests would render our getaway a failure, but instead it seemed to enhance the reputations of those involved. It reminded me of the unexpected burning down of my would-be party place. I guess surviving disaster has its advantages.

Legendary partier status, of course, came at a higher price for Gabe and Fat Juan.

Gabe's well-educated older sister was already a well-placed attorney within Arizona's legal system, but it took her two days to get him out of jail and back home. Fat Juan's family had fewer resources, so they had to let him live the life of a jailbird two days longer. Then of course, they had fines and arrest records to worry about.

I, for once, had the good fortune to simply remember it all rather fondly. How could I not? Whenever I pass through Payson, I still stop for gas at my favorite station, the one with the trademark wooden Indian. I suspect I'm one of their only customers with an intimate understanding of why it is now securely bolted into place.

ABOUT THAT CAT

M y friend Bob was typical of many cat lovers who argue that their pets are somehow superior to their canine counterparts. I grew up with a desert menagerie which featured all manner of wildlife, domesticated and otherwise, and it was clear that the dogs were far more intelligent than the cats. Bob shouldn't have been defensive about that simple fact, because his cat was smarter than my grandpa's parakeet, which was smarter than my little sister's goldfish, and so on.

Since dogs were smarter, you could have more fun with them. That was the whole point. Goldfish were too dumb to play with, but they were wonderfully low maintenance. Most of us simply accepted that our assorted pets were meant to satisfy different needs and appreciated them for that.

Not so for Bob and his fellow cat lovers. They persisted with an argument that was essentially the same as an organ grinder insisting to a parent that his monkey was just as smart as their eight-year-old child. That silly argument so irritated the non-cat owners who heard it that they finally began to vent their frustrations.

The fuss gave rise to a cottage industry that produced dead cat books, T-shirts, and wall hangings. That was unfortunate. Cats got a bad rap and they deserved better. While dogs were my personal favorite, I always enjoyed cats. I even liked Bob's cat— especially after it got run over.

As desert kids, we had to manufacture our own fun. We couldn't ride our skateboards to the nearest mall and its video arcade. The nearest mall was forty miles away. There were no sidewalks, and we had no skateboards. In this environment, no opportunity for entertainment went unexplored, including dead animals on the roadway.

One should not assume this form of rural recreation was without its redeeming qualities. Danny Boorman kept a group of us enthralled one afternoon while dissecting a coyote that lost an argument with a semi-truck. Danny now has a successful medical practice in the Bay Area.

Cats, however, were the best. Thanks to "sailcatting,"a desert tradition as old as pavement itself, a single dead cat could yield hours of safe, inexpensive entertainment.

Preparing a proper sailcat required patience. After repeated passing cars flattened the cat and plastered it firmly to the highway, you had to allow the sun a few days to dry and cure the carcass. When the cat looked and felt like hairy beef jerky, it was time to pry it up and let the fur fly.

No kid could fling a flattened feline quite like Conrad Givens. He could do things with a sailcat that would make any modern day Frisbee master stand up and take notice. I can still picture him carefully assessing a specimen. He would gently wobble the sailcat up and down for a bit, gauging its unique characteristics. A sailcat's weight was never evenly distributed, nor was its circumference perfectly symmetrical. This meant every flight of fancy took its own unpredictable course.

When Conrad sent Bob's former pet skyward it proved to be a "splitter," which meant that, at the peak of its arc, it separated into three pieces. This is to sailcatting what the grand finale is to a fireworks display.

After high school, the most inspired act associated with a dead cat I have ever witnessed was executed by Jim Tandy, and it had nothing to do with the kid's stuff of sailcatting.

Everything about Jim Tandy was big and he was generally outspoken. He was tall and just heavy enough to sport a starter gut. If Jim was loud, his truck, powered by an enormous V8, qualified as particularly loud. His purchase of the biggest, fastest truck in the area was meant to impress the girls. But most girls, even the ones who messed around, wanted no part of big Jim—especially not *that* part.

I, however, enjoyed Jim's company. He had a brutally sarcastic wit and idea of him on a double date seemed like guaranteed fun..

Eventually my girlfriend, Lisa, convinced her friend, Karen, to round out a foursome for us. Karen was from Phoenix, which, by rural standards, made her sophisticated and mysterious. We had yet to realize that her neighborhood of West Phoenix was a cultural wasteland and that our awe was without merit. I was simply happy that Karen was from someplace else and didn't know better than to go out with Jim.

We were seated four abreast in Jim's truck, making the one-hour drive to Phoenix for a cheap dinner and a movie. The journey required crawling through a dusty little speed trap where the main street would have been completely without distinction were it not for the immensely large dead cat that adorned it.

Jim and I made several crude comments appropriate to the situation and thought that would be the end of it. But no, our dates had other ideas.

"Go back and get it out of the road," they whined in unison.

We laughed, hoping our suggestion that they were kidding would get them to drop the subject.

"Nooooo," they continued, "really you guys, we can't just leave it there. Go back! Pleeeeease." My God, they were serious.

I was trying to think of how best to get our dates off the subject of the ill-fated feline when Jim did the most unexpected thing. He stopped his truck, put it in reverse, and started backing up toward the dead cat.

I could not believe it. I was about to protest when I realized this date must have really been important to Jim. Karen had no way of knowing what an outrageous goof Jim Tandy could be and perhaps he wanted to keep it that way for as long as possible. I almost felt sorry for him, definitely disgusted, but almost sorry.

Our dates, of course, were delighted. They beamed with the satisfaction young women get only from manipulating young men.

Their expressions changed when they realized Jim had brought the left rear tire of his truck to rest squarely atop that bloated dead cat. Their eyes widened and their mouths slowly dropped open as Jim revved the powerful engine to a thunderous roar. I felt ashamed of myself for ever doubting him.

The back of the truck sank down as Jim dropped it into gear, causing the rear tires to spin in place with ferocious velocity, emitting a deafening, almost demonic, high-pitched squeal.

Jim finally threw the transmission back into neutral and we sat there for a moment, letting the shroud of blue-gray smoke clear from around the panting vehicle.

Our dates were not merely shocked, but quite literally *in shock*. Their normally healthy, sun-tanned faces were now pasty white and looked clammy. I regret that, because the subtle mock sincerity of what Jim delivered next was completely wasted on them.

"There," he said, "it's out of the road."

Never before had I written off the prospect of recreational sex so early on a date, and never before had it been so worth it.

YUKS ON THE POND

I learned at an early age that complaining to my parents about the harsh indignities of a desert upbringing was futile.

Since they were also raised on the American Outback, their pat response to my problem *du jour* was abjectly unsympathetic: "It's good for you, it will build character." I wanted to respond with, "Sure, those pygmies running around naked in the Brazilian rainforest are probably brimming with character, but I wouldn't want to be one of them." Yep, that's how I wanted to respond, but I usually thought better of it.

The degree of self-sufficiency demanded of those living in the middle of nowhere was extreme. No city services meant extra cold showers if you forgot to have the gas company send a truck to refill your propane fuel tank. Of course, you might be denied a shower, cold or otherwise, if the proverbial well ran dry. That occurred every seven years or so and prompted Dad to call a team of large, leather-skinned men from Buttcrack Central. These guys would come out and further sink our well to reach the ever-receding underground aquifer.

In the desert, no cranky trash men came around in growling trucks to take our refuse away. And eventually, the Environmental Protection Agency outlawed the fun of weekly trash burning. That forced us to haul our fifty-gallon drums of discards to a festering pit in a remote stretch of the desert. On hot summer afternoons, the stench of that pit would ride a desert breeze for miles.

As it turned out, my parents were right. Getting involved in the character-building maintenance of *El Rancho Remoto* left all their children wise beyond their years. Consequently, we were entrusted with grown up responsibilities at a relatively tender age.

Each summer my parents embraced their only indulgence–our family cabin in the mountains of central Arizona. Dad went to join my Mom and the younger kids every weekend, leaving me to look after our sweltering homestead during my most formative summers.

Of course, I did all the stupid stuff you would expect of a hormonally charged adolescent, but with the tact common only to teenagers of enhanced character. Sure, there were parties, but not the over-the-top free-for-alls thrown by kids who rarely got the opportunity to play host. My gatherings were more sophisticated affairs. It was as if *Playboy After Dark* were being staged in Hooterville. True to character, I meticulously cleaned up on the morning after.

It was, however, far more common for me to entertain a friend alone. The Bull Dogger was littered with good-hearted, wanton women. They afforded me ample opportunity to sow my wild oats. Over a few fun-filled summers, I must have sown enough wild oats to send the hungry inhabitants of a Third World country to bed fat and happy.

Even in the vigorous pursuit of vice, the virtue of my character came into play. While it was hardly fashionable during the mid-70s, I always used what we discretely referred to as "protection." I didn't want an unplanned pregnancy (and at age seventeen, is there any other kind?) embarrassing my extended rural family or altering my carefully crafted career plans.

My preventative maintenance paid dividends. A few years later, I was gainfully employed in my chosen field and living in a booming city four hundred miles from home. My parents were thrilled. Like my brother before me, I had transcended the paycheck-to-paycheck existence that led most young wage earners to darken their parent's doorstep the first time an unforeseen expense exceeded their cash flows. By rural standards, this made us unqualified overachievers.

So it was with much pride that I returned home one spring weekend to pay my respects and lend a hand with one of those character-building ordeals unique to life in the sticks. My parent's septic tank was full and needed to be pumped out. I helped shovel away the dirt from a twelve-by-twelve foot area that entombed the vile concrete vessel. As the hydraulic arm of a backhoe lifted the lid from the septic tank, the faint-hearted half of my family retreated to the safety of the house. The rest of us stayed to watch, drawn by the same morbid curiosity that causes people to slow down and look at automobile accidents.

Once the lid of the septic tank was lifted, I was abruptly reminded of my responsibly reckless youth. It seems condoms have roughly the same half-life as plutonium—and they float. I was shocked by how well they float. In the unlikely event of a water landing, forget using your seat cushion as a flotation device. Instead, just wrap yourself in prophylactics and your buoyancy is guaranteed.

Suddenly all eyes were trained on me. Even the anonymous backhoe operator shut down his engine, ensuring an awkward silence to compliment my painfully obvious blushing. My six-year-old baby sister finally broke the silence by pointing at the rubber regatta undulating on the murky surface by exclaiming, "Look! Balloons!"

I turned to my younger brother whose face could scarcely contain his grin and asked, "Would you please take her in the house?" He dutifully led her away, but not before she extended her tiny arm and offered one last observation, "Hey, there's a blue one!"

When they were safely out of earshot, my dad took his turn. "A blue one?" He continued before I could reply, "You know Greg, if she were old enough to understand this, you'd have some explaining to do."

"Yeah, Dad, I suppose." I waited a beat before continuing, "But then again, if she were old enough to understand this, it would be a great character lesson, too."

THE BINGO GIGOLOS

The Las Vegas I moved to at the tender age of nineteen was much different from the pricey, corporate-controlled, multigenerational theme park it later became. The Vegas of the mid-seventies was a much smaller city, still under mob control, and with a greater emphasis on glamour.

People dressed up before entering the casinos in those days and collectively lost big enough for gaming proceeds to subsidize all the other mesmerizing aspects of Sin City. As a result, lavish rooms, elegant buffets, and spectacular stage shows could all be enjoyed at bargain prices. It was a formula that worked.

Some hapless electrician from Ohio might put on his Sunday best and pretend he was Sean Connery before getting clobbered at the craps table. Those other well-priced amenities, however, left a good overall impression of Lost Wages and made him anxious to return.

Taking advantage of those cheap amenities was one of the great benefits of being a local, particularly if you didn't underwrite those amenities by being an aggressive gambler. For me, getting to know that unique local aspect of Las Vegas, while also getting to know a brand new job, was as confusing as it was cool.

Just six-months earlier I was working as a staff artist in the news department of the NBC affiliate in Phoenix. On a whim, I decided to drive to Boulder City, Nevada, to visit my grandparents. Since Las Vegas lay just forty-five minutes to the north, I also made time to call on Pat Turney, the promotion manager of the local CBS affiliate. The station was still so small that Pat farmed their graphic design needs out to a local freelancer, but I still found my meeting with the high-energy eccentric completely enjoyable. That's why I was so excited when he called a short time later to explain that his little empire had just expanded to include a one-person art department. Given the increase in responsibility, title, and salary, we agreed that person should be me.

So I became an employee of KLAS TV, a small station owned by Howard Hughes. It sat in the shadow of his penthouse apartment atop the Desert Inn Hotel, just off the Las Vegas strip. My little ground floor apartment in the shadow of the Las Vegas Hilton was just a bicycle ride away from work. The Hilton was also home to, what was by then, the bloated version of Elvis.

I found it all fascinating, but as mentioned, also a bit overwhelming. It became much easier when I met Todd Ruffalo.

By this time, I was pretty immune to homesickness. But still, it was nice when Todd introduced himself and suggested we grab a beer.

Todd was born in Philly but had grown up in Las Vegas. That was about as close to a native Las Vegan as you were likely to find back then. He was a walking contradiction. Actually, he shuffled more than he walked—and with a slouch at that. Plus, he was quiet and laid back to the point of seeming unmotivated and apathetic. On the contrary, Todd was exceptionally good at everything he decided was worth doing. He was an outstanding athlete, a studio-grade musician, and those in the know considered him one of the brighter people at the station.

Getting established as Todd's friend offered many advantages. He knew lots of interesting people, the ins-and-out of the city, and he even taught me enough about gambling that I didn't feel completely lost if I wandered into a casino. Being Todd's friend also meant getting used to him dropping by my apartment unannounced, as he did one hot Saturday afternoon in June. "Whatcha doing?" he asked, in lieu of a greeting.

"Nothing, really," I responded. "What's going on?"

"Nothing," he said. "Let's go get a beer."

"I can't, Todd," I said. "My beer budget is all tapped out."

This prompted an eye roll from Todd, which was about as demonstrative as he was likely to get. His exasperation stemmed from the fact that he knew I had money in my wallet. I did, however, observe a budget and it included money for socializing. But, I had just hosted a saucy little soiree the previous weekend and didn't want to blow any more money on partying until the next payday. Since Todd was present at that sparkling affair I didn't expect him to protest too much, but he pressed on any way. "Okay, Dog Lips," he asked, "have you got three dollars?"

"Yes," I said, "but—"

"Then shut up and come with me," he interrupted.

While climbing into Todd's new, light yellow Monte Carlo, I made a mental note to surprise him with a lime green mohair dash cover. Given that retirees and urban sex trade moguls were the only other people who drove those homely, low-slung cars, it was all he needed to round out the pimpmobile quality of his ride.

As Todd drove I enjoyed the view of uninspired, semi-industrial architecture that filled the nowhere land between the strip and downtown Las Vegas. Because he was a local, he was able to navigate downtown's nooks and crannies like a Celestial traversing the crowded, narrow alleyways of a big city's China Town.

Finally, after we parked and got out of the car, Todd led me through a maze of walkways and unassuming buildings before he pulled open a plain metal door and pushed me out of the bright sunlight and into the dim, smoky air of a large room. He continued to push me forward until I bumped into a metal framed chair. I reached down and could feel that it had an upholstered seat and back. As I settled into it, my eyes began to adjust to their new surroundings.

There were long, narrow tables arranged in an orderly fashion. Women sat around these tables—exclusively. It would be generous to describe the youngest of them as middle-aged. Most had one hand cocked aloft, gently cradling a neglected cigarette while they tried to steal glances at us without losing track of the bingo cards spread out before them. I leaned toward Todd and inquired quietly through clinched teeth, "What are we doing here?"

"Shut up," he whispered back, "get out your lousy three bucks, buy one beer, two bingo cards, and follow my lead."

I was hardly in a position to argue, so I did as he ordered. Given the concentration I needed to keep up with placing little wooden discs over the called-out numbers, I had trouble taking in all that was happening around me. Being super-human, it must have been easier for Todd to play bingo while also chatting up the half-dozen old gals who were within easy earshot of us. There were, however, a few details I was able to ascertain. All these ladies were local and they were regulars. This weekly ritual not only allowed for socializing, but it also offered escape from the afternoon temperatures building up in their single-wide trailer homes.

At last, someone screamed "BINGO!" Then Todd pushed back from the table, stretched, and said, "Thank you, ladies. It's been a pleasure."

A near riot ensued, driven by a chorus of questions and demands. "What?!? What's the rush!?! Sit down!!! Somebody bring these boys another drink!!!"

I didn't even have time to stand up before a burst of applause broke out as Todd reclaimed his seat. Within seconds, there were fresh bingo cards and three beers each splayed out before us.

Only then did I realize what was happening. Todd Ruffalo had put me squarely on the path toward some twisted form of male prostitution. The worst part was this—I liked it.

Our exchanges over the next few hours were actually more familial than flirtatious. It was as if these ladies were not getting enough interaction from their absentee sons or grandsons, and we were deemed acceptable surrogates.

Hours later, we staggered out the door along with many of our fellow bingo players, utterly happy and completely buzzed. The glow of neon made it difficult to discern the time, but the cooler temperatures suggested early evening.

I giggled and shook my head as Todd and I made our way toward downtown's Fremont Street. Waiting to cross, I took in the ribbon of backlit marquees surrounding Benny Binion's Horseshoe club. The big, red, plastic letters on one of them read, "T-Bone Steak Dinner $2.99."

"C'mon," I said. "I'm buying."

THE BRITISH ARE COMING!

It would have been an utterly forgettable spring morning were it not for the pout on Sally Johnson's face as she walked into the art department. Her usual combination of laid back energy and an easy smile made her welcome everywhere at KLVX, a small PBS station where I worked in Las Vegas, Nevada. Since Sally's smile was nowhere in evidence, I pushed back from my drawing table and asked, "What's up?"

"I think I need your help," Sally responded.

That was when I first learned about the Friendship Force. In the late 1970s, First Lady Rosalynn Carter decided to improve cultural understanding between the United States and other countries by extending the concept of foreign exchange students to adults. The plan was simple: take a planeload of Americans from a place like Kansas City and fly them to a place like Madrid, then refill that plane with Spaniards and fly them back to Kansas City. Adults traveling each way were responsible for arranging host families for their foreign counterparts to stay with during the two week program. Sally had been accepted in the program and in a few days would be on a plane full of Las Vegans en route to the city of New Castle in the north of England.

"Sounds brilliant," I said. "So why the long face?"

"I'm having second thoughts about using my parents as my host family." Sally said, still looking tense.

In spite of her anglicized name, Sally Johnson was a full-blooded Navajo Indian and her parents still lived on the reservation where she grew up near the Colorado River outside of Parker, Arizona.

I studied Sally for a moment before asking, "Are you sure, Sally? People can come to Vegas most any time and it will pretty much be the same. But a chance to experience real Native American culture is a unique opportunity."

Sally countered with, "It sounds nice when you say like that, Greg. But two weeks of fry bread and sweat lodges compared to Wayne Newton, fabulous showgirls, and all-you-can-eat buffets?" Her quiet, monotone delivery of what sounded like something off a chamber of commerce flyer made me smile, and seconds later we were both laughing.

"Fair enough," I said. "But how can I help?"

Her response surprised me. She said, "I was hoping you and Lucy could be my host family. You're both young, you don't have children, and you're more fun than anyone else around this place."

Lucy and I were still newlyweds. Maybe my rookie status as a husband was among the reasons I accepted Sally's request without first checking with my wife, but luckily, Lucy's reaction to the news confirmed my hunch that she would love the idea of us playing host to people from an interesting, faraway place. I based my hunch on the fact that Lucy always had a fun-loving spirit, which was one of the things that first attracted me to her. Back when I met her, she was always at the center of the weekend parties that seemed a constant in her family's huge desert hacienda. Since we got married and she moved to Las Vegas, her opportunities for such gaiety had greatly diminished. Adding to her enthusiasm was Sally's assurance that we would be matched up with our visiting family based on age and interests, so really, what could go wrong?

Our excitement gave way to concern when we tried to look at our home with the fresh, discerning eyes of foreign visitors. The phrases, "starter home," "fixer-upper," "needing TLC," all applied in spades to our modest fifties era, two-bedroom, cinder block, no-style ranch style home. It would have been one thing if ours was the lone fixer-upper on an otherwise good street in a promising neighborhood. But that wasn't the case. Our whole neighborhood was on the brink of sliding into a depressed state from which it might not recover. Its fate depended on whether other young couples like us moved in and fixed up their homes before moving on. These were not, however, the kinds of problems that could be dealt with in a couple of days, so we simply prioritized a list of things we could tackle inside our house and hoped for the best.

Two nights later, we made our way into a local high school auditorium where we tried to play catch-up at the last official Freedom Force meeting on the eve of the arrival of the Vegas-bound Brits. At the front of the auditorium there were a dozen middle-aged people seated at folding tables flipping intently through three-ring binders. I found someone who seemed interested in my desire to get squared away as Sally Johnson's replacement host family and he handed me a sealed envelope. I found my seat next to Lucy before opening it. I quickly looked it over and giggled nervously before reading it aloud for Lucy. "We're getting a 68-year-old widow named Gertrude Fallon. She likes Agatha Christie mysteries and needle point."

"So much for getting matched up by age and interest," laughed Lucy. "Maybe Gertrude was already matched for Sally's parents."

That's when we were interrupted by a polite, barely audible, "Excuse me." Only then did I notice the lovely older lady seated in front of us. She twisted around as best she could to face us. "Excuse me," she repeated, "but I couldn't help but overhear you young people and wondered if you would be interested in trading for my 26-year-olds? He likes to play golf and she enjoys nightlife. I don't golf," she deadpanned, leaving open the possibility that she, too, enjoys a little nightlife now and then.

Lucy and I thought about it for all of two seconds; then, like kids on the playground swapping dog-eared baseball cards, we traded our Gertrude Fallon for her Frank and Haley Gordon. The Friendship Force coordinators, seriously going about their business at the front of the room, were none the wiser.

Perhaps it was the quick guest trade with our elderly friend from the auditorium that denied us contact information for our guests; but even if we had it, time zone considerations would have complicated connecting with our soon-to-be house guests.

As with the other Friendship Force families, we showed up at McCarran Airport at the appointed time, ready to greet the guests we had yet to speak with. As we waited with the other host families, it became apparent just how different that made us from them. Clearly, those around us had exchanged photos and correspondence weeks in advance of this day. Other than their respective interests in golf and nightlife, we knew nothing of the

Gordons. So we waited for them to exit the plane and enter the terminal as I held high a posterboard with their names on it.

Whatever the leap of faith Lucy and I were taking, it was minuscule compared the one undertaken by Frank and Haley. They sat on a plane, knowing nothing of the family they were destined for, or for that matter, if a family actually waited for them at all.

Shortly thereafter, like two armies rushing toward each other on a battlefield, the Brits and the Yanks collided. Instead of hand-to-hand combat, there were hugs and laughter. Perhaps none of those giddy embraces were more enthusiastic than those between us and the Gordons, because the four of us enjoyed the collective relief that we had not been duped into some complex international practical joke.

Amidst the hugs and excitement, we managed to steal glances at one another. Haley was lovely in a zaftig kind of way, and her maroon-tinted hair and hipster attire embodied all I knew of British Mod. It was Frank's appearance, however, that offered the biggest surprise for me. At a distance, we could pass for one another. We were roughly the same height and build. We both wore glasses, our hair was very similar in style and color, and we both sported full beards. I had to fight the urge to make my first words to him, "My, but you're a handsome fellow!"

Lucy wasn't so discerning. We had hardly navigated our 1968 VW Squareback away from the airport when she told them soberly, "You can relax with us. We don't drink or carry on. You're in for a quiet, relaxing visit to Las Vegas." The Gordons nodded politely just before Lucy squealed, "Just kidding! Who wants LV?" LV was her favorite concoction, a mixture of frozen lemonade and vodka. Unbeknownst to me, she had prepared a gallon of it and stowed it, along with plastic cups, in the car before we left the house. The party was on, and it didn't let up for the next two weeks.

One of First Lady Rosalynn Carter's hoped-for benefits of this cultural exchange was that visitors would have experiences they could only get while staying with locals rather than in the homogenous world of major hotels. And that happened for the Gordons in a variety of little ways. They warmed to the sweets (pancakes) we served for breakfast. They were horrified at the mind-numbing barrage of commercials that cluttered our television and radio waves. And they were confused at the way Americans had bastardized the Queen's English once we got it a safely away from the British shores.

We had to decipher words with alternate meanings, like jumper, knickers, and yard. They had to explain other slang terms to us that don't normally surface here, like brekkie, brally, and shag. Lucy and I were soon parroting new phrases and even picking up hints of the British accent. My personal favorite was something Frank said when a situation met with his approval, and being a positive sort, he said it a lot: "That's good, that."

Lucy wasn't yet working, so she could play Vegas tour guide throughout the day. I hadn't accrued much vacation time, so I mostly joined our guests at night. Fortunately, at twenty-three, I still had the stamina needed for a handful of all-nighters.

Because this was at the time when gambling still bankrolled most everything in Vegas, there were stage shows, food, and drinks to be had at bargain prices. We took advantage of all of it.

One of our best episodes of bargain entertainment played out in the wee hours of the morning while we were carousing on the strip. We were sitting in a club called Paul Anka's Sinsation.

Paul Anka was typical of that subset of veteran entertainers who enjoyed a last hurrah in Las Vegas. It made sense. The visitors who patronized Vegas back then were older and less diverse than they are today. If this crowd wanted to recapture its lost youth, why not do it with those who provided the soundtrack they listened to while they were wasting that youth in the first place?

In another respect, Paul Anka was unique from other entertainment elephants that lumbered into the Vegas boneyard to die, because he actually enjoyed a modest comeback with a song entitled "Having My Baby." I've always tried not to be ageist in my observations, but this song always creeped me out. The image of this artificially preserved senior citizen coupling with anyone young enough to support a viable pregnancy was not one I wanted in my head. Still, his nightclub was cool, and on this particular evening we were quite pleased to be in it, drinking and dancing the night away.

Around 2 A.M. I was thinking of asking Lucy to join me for one last dance when I suddenly felt uncomfortable. It took me a moment to realize that my reluctance to hit the dance floor was born of insecurity. I simply didn't feel I was good enough to be out there. By most standards, Lucy and I were good dancers and we'd been happily on the dance floor for most of the evening. At this point, however, I was either getting really wasted, or the dancers we were watching had just gotten an awful lot better. Frank weighed in, "You may well be wasted, but either way, these dancers are fantastic—good looking, too."

He was right. It was as though a collection of super models and Solid Gold Dancers were tossed into a blender and the silky smooth result had been poured onto Sinsation's dance floor. Our cocktail waitress then explained that the last of the stage shows had just finished and this was where a lot of performers came to wind down on the way home from work. Only in Las Vegas...

In no time at all the Gordons' visit came to an end, but our relationship had just begun, particularly where Frank and I were concerned. Over the three decades since our unlikely introduction, our friendship has remained a constant. It outlasted our marriages to Haley and Lucy and it expanded to include others. Many of my stateside friends and family became close to Frank, just as I gained a number of wonderful friends in England through my connection with him.

Through it all, I've found Frank to be remarkably durable. He endured heat stroke on the golf course, fireworks mishaps in Mexico, and desert toad explorations in rural farm country with me. We rode treacherous canyon roads in an old truck held together with duct tape and bungee cords, and later played amateur detective trying to figure out where the hell we left that old truck before the previous night's festivities magically transported us miles away from it.

Since this expanse of time, my work has taken me from Las Vegas back to my home town of Phoenix, then west to Los Angeles, north to San Francisco, and ultimately further north to my current home in a small town on the California Delta. Frank has visited me at least once in each of these places, and I've had the pleasure of visiting him a few times in Newcastle, as well. Still, there remained an inequity in our travel efforts, with Frank visiting me twice for every once I've visited him. When I tried to explain this away, I suggested that we Yanks don't get nearly as much vacation time as our more civilized allies across the pond. Frank easily conceded that point, which only added to my defensiveness. So then I pointed out the absolute necessity of escaping the deep freeze that passes for winter in the north of England and suggested that I moved from one interesting city to the next, all with wonderful winter weather, largely with his needs in mind. Again, Frank agreed, the merciless bastard.

The obvious fact is that Frank has done a better job of supporting the friendship than I have. This is just one of many shortcomings for which he has forgiven me. I guess that's what friends do.

The Friendship Force is still alive and well and I sometimes wonder what first lady Rosalynn Carter would think of what we've done with the opportunity she made possible. I suspect she would sum it up much as Frank does—with a hearty, "That's good, that."

THE EYES HAVE IT

My thirteen years of employment at KPHO TV back in Phoenix couldn't have been more gratifying. It was, particularly when I first arrived there, one of the most successful independent television stations in the country. I liked my co-workers and so enjoyed the work that I didn't even notice the long hours I put in. My bosses did notice, however, and they rewarded me with promotions. When I was promoted from art director to the station's head of marketing, the change was easy for me—it simply presented a bigger creative challenge. A couple of years later, when they asked me to oversee the programming department, it was a much greater adjustment. Suddenly my job had gone from highly creative to largely analytical. But I figured what the hell—if I didn't like it I could always go back to the creative side of things, either there or at some other station.

I didn't just enjoy programming—I loved it. Because independent television stations traded in kids' shows, reruns of off-network television series, and older movies, maybe it seemed like a less glamorous place to ply one's trade, but I found that just the opposite was true. KPHO not only traded in the very best of the rerun programming, but it also produced more local programming than its local network-affiliated rivals. In addition to local newscasts, the station produced a robust kid's program and a local talk show. It also presented hosted movies and award-winning documentaries.

Overseeing the station's locally produced programming seemed a natural extension of the creative responsibilities I'd already known. But this job also made me responsible for negotiating deals to get those all-important reruns, movies, and cartoons. That not only required more strategic and financial planning, but it also meant that I had to learn to become one with the beast—more specifically, I needed to become a *broadcast executive.*

Fortunately, office behavior was improving quickly during that time both at our station and throughout the broadcast industry. When I first arrived at KPHO, sexual harassment was not only tolerated, but it was an acceptable management style. "Joe here is a stern taskmaster, Bill is a great consensus builder, and Larry, well—he is an exceptionally good horn-dog."

By the time I took over programming, our general manager had largely addressed the harassment problem by outlawing what he referred to as "fishing off the company pier."

Even with sexual intrigue on the wane, there was plenty of behavior that, though it was routine back then, seems utterly foreign now. Smokers, for instance, didn't step outside for a cigarette; instead non-smokers were forced outside for a breath of fresh air. You might have a drink at lunch if you didn't mind being called a weak-assed wimp, otherwise you would get with the spirit of things and have three or four drinks, like everybody else. Nobody thought twice about climbing behind the wheel of the big company car and driving the rest of the half-drunk management team back to the office. It was in this environment that I learned to negotiate programming deals.

Because most stations enjoyed large profit margins, they had ample budgets for programming purchases, and as a result, the program suppliers enjoyed plenty of well-funded customers.

While the stations did well, the program suppliers did ever better. Before ever going into reruns, most sitcoms and drama series had been paid for by the national networks that originally aired them. That meant the money from selling them into local markets was essentially gravy, multiplied by nearly two hundred local markets. That's a lot of gravy. The same held true for movie packages that had already recouped most of their initial production costs at the box office.

Those who sold these programs to people like me at the local television stations were called syndicators. They were generally well paid, well dressed, and very well versed at getting the most out of their generous expense accounts. They stayed at the best hotels, took their customers to the finest restaurants, and treated us to golf at the most exclusive resorts. This was all under the pretense of getting a deal done.

To be clear, there was plenty of hard work happening in conjunction with the high-flying frivolity. Many of the long hours we spent on the details of running the business were anything but glamorous. Still, I was always struck with the inequity inherent in the system. For most people working in broadcasting, it was nothing but long hours of hard work with very few of the perks unique to that exclusive fraternity of buyers and sellers.

This inequity was best displayed at NATPE, the annual programming convention put on by the National Association of Television Program Executives. I always had trouble keeping that acronym straight in my head until a more experienced programmer suggested, "think insect urine."

Even amidst the lavish entertaining that was the hallmark of NATPE, plenty of business got done. Most would concede, however, that the primary purpose of the convention was for broadcasters to reward themselves for their wildly profitable year and for the syndication community to say thank you for the business.

It would be hard to exaggerate the lengths to which the program suppliers went to express that gratitude. At its peak, NATPE was attracting twenty thousand buyers from around the world. There was support staff from hundreds of program suppliers adding thousands more to the attendance totals. Then there was media representation ranging from local entertainment writers to national trade journalists to the team from *Entertainment Tonight*. They were all on hand to document the affair.

An exhibition of this size could only be held in cities with venues capable of handling the biggest conventions, with Las Vegas and New Orleans getting a lion's share of the bookings. Within cavernous convention halls, the major program suppliers erected massive structures wherein they entertained their customers. All the food and drink anyone could want awaited those who wandered in. Celebrities were on hand for meet-and-greets and to pose for photos with prospective buyers. Smaller studios and production companies filled in the acres of real estate between the monuments of the behemoth entertainment companies. It was all spectacularly excessive.

Nowhere was the excess more evident than in the area of giveaways. These free items would later be called "premiums" and, ultimately, "swag." Almost every program that was taken to market had its name emblazoned across some form of apparel, jewelry, toy, or sporting good. The annual haul for freebie-grubbing buyers was so immense that some of them started taking empty suit cases to NATPE to make it easier to transport their loot home. Many enterprising syndicators saw the opportunity in this, so they started embroidering their logos on luggage to give away at the convention.

Again, while many of us enjoyed these spoils, there were many people who were just as deserving but were largely excluded. For me, the best example of someone who deserved to be at the party was Donny Unitas. His name may as well have been Donny Not-the-Famous-Quarterback-Johnny-Unitas, for that is how he was usually introduced. Not that anyone would confuse Donny for a professional athlete, not even one long since retired. He was pudgy, bespectacled, balding, and always dressed in a manner reflective of his conservative Midwestern roots. More importantly, he was a charming orator, a brilliant attorney, and one of the funniest people I had ever met.

After I negotiated the broad strokes of a programming purchase—price, term, and plays—it was Donny's job to comb through the voluminous long form contract and then call me to follow up on any fine print that ran contrary to the spirit of the agreement. We usually scheduled these calls at times that allowed us to quickly work though the necessary contract discussions so we would have time to discuss our favorite television shows. Being a videophile was a requirement of my job, but for Donny, it was a born-in passion. We had good fun comparing thoughts on the latest episodes of *St. Elsewhere* or *Northern Exposure*, but by the time *Seinfeld* was on our collective radar, I was leaving KPHO for the west coast and a then little-known cable network called E! Entertainment Television.

My years of programming at KPHO had been fun and enlightening, but the business was changing rapidly in a way that could only be described as "diminishing returns." By the early 1990s, the Neilsen ratings books that crossed my desk reflected viewership that was in free fall. The declining ratings were in direct proportion to another statistic that was on the rise: cable penetration. "Penetrated" is just how the local station operators felt, because for each household that discovered the joys of Nickelodeon, MTV, ESPN, and HBO, their viewing of local stations dropped considerably.

At E!, I found a young organization that held an appeal similar to that of my early days at KPHO, because it was a network looking to create its own brand and its own original programming in the growth industry that was then cable television. With my learning curve again arching upward, and with buying off-network programming as a much smaller part of my job, I decided to pass on attending that particular year's NATPE convention. But then I received a most unexpected, but welcomed, phone call.

My good friend Donny Unitas was finally getting to attend NATPE and wondered if I was going to be there. I said, "I am now," and I asked my assistant to book me a room in Las Vegas, where that year's convention was being held.

While NATPE was beginning to fade in much the same way the local broadcast business had, it was still a big exhibition. That, coupled with a major home builder convention hitting town at the same time, meant there were no rooms available in the city. I had lived in Las Vegas for several years as a younger man and found it hard to believe the entire city was booked. I calmly and confidently told my assistant to check downtown, as it would be off the radar of many attendees. "Already checked everything downtown," she said, "but I'm still working on it." Then, I started to get nervous.

Hours later, my assistant returned saying that, just as she was about give up, she got a lead on a motel on North Las Vegas Boulevard called the Sulinda. I asked her to repeat the address and tried to recall that stretch of the strip. "That's north of the Sahara," I said. "There is nothing up there but dive diners, pawn shops, and a few hooker hotels." She looked at me wide-eyed, realizing the magnitude of my decision. This was Las Vegas after all, where "hooker hotel" wasn't simply a euphemism for downmarket accommodations, but literally an establishment where patrons were more likely to pay for their rooms by the hour than the evening.

"Book it," I said.

"This Donny Unitas must be somebody really important," she replied.

I thought about it for a moment and said, "He is at that."

A few nights later in Las Vegas, I addressed the first item of my hastily prepared NATPE agenda. What I thought would be a quiet dinner with a few cable syndicators turned into a longer, crazier night than I expected.

Based on my knowledge of the two gentlemen who had invited me out, I was expecting an enjoyable, but relatively quiet dinner and perhaps a few drinks. Since, however, they knew we were going to be seated at a table for four, they also invited a former associate who had struck out on his own. He was a nice enough guy, but he was also much louder and more amped up than the rest of us. After a great dinner at the restaurant atop the Horseshoe club, I was looking forward to a brief nightcap and getting on to whatever challenges awaited me at the Sulinda. The moment we exited the hotel's street level casino, however, our fourth man, Mr. High Energy, made a beeline for the Gaslight, a downtown strip club, drawing us all along in his wake.

Lest I come off as a complete hypocrite, I'll admit that I am not opposed to an occasional visit to any of the finer topless dives a convention city might have to offer. That stated, I have done this enough to know that the initial excitement of seeing an attractive young woman prance about topless quickly wears off and leaves a "What now?" awkwardness afterward. For that reason, I am only comfortable hitting these places with close friends who, like me, prefer to hang at a table in the back where we can quietly crack wise about the absurdities playing out before us. That wasn't an option with Mr. High Energy leading the way. He beamed with pride as he muscled his way to the center of the club, which he now referred to as the Asslight, and secured us four seats at the foot of the dancer's runway.

Sitting in such a conspicuous section of a topless club is rife with problems. The first problem is shear awkwardness. Some of these young women have deluded themselves into thinking they are performing on the fringes of traditional dance rather than at the core of the adult entertainment industry. As such, they make eye contact and smile as though everything is perfectly normal. It is difficult to respond in kind, however, when your entertainer is gyrating just three feet away from you clad in nothing but knee-high vinyl boots and a matching G-string. Even worse are those dancers who embrace their roles as adult entertainers and muster expressions of unbridled lust during their performances. The idea that these attractive young women could be turned on by the array of puffy, florid faces perspiring before them exceeds even my own well-developed ability to suspend disbelief.

The other problem with sitting at the runway concerns tipping. The price one pays for a perspective usually afforded only to significant others, and gynecologists, is an offering of folded currency at the end of each dance. It's not that I begrudge these young ladies their tips. In fact, whether they return home to a dorm room at UNLV, or to a mobile home-cum-meth lab in North Las Vegas, I think they deserve every dollar they can get. It's just that the delivery of a tip compounds the issue of awkward interaction at best, and can lead to more serious ramifications at worst.

There are easily six means of tip transfer common to most topless bars, but I'll focus only on the three that were in play on the night I reluctantly visited the Gaslight. The first technique is relatively harmless and is known as "the sweep." With this maneuver, a patron simply pushes a piece of currency out onto the section of dance floor directly in front of him. As the action is almost completely benign, my issue with the sweep has more to do with style than substance. Maybe it's just the television producer in me, but having a dancer stooping over picking up tips when the next dancer should be charging into the spotlight seems like an unnecessary break in the flow of a performance. It is also undignified for a dancer, who should be allowed to bask in the applause of an appreciative audience rather than scurry about the stage like a young mother picking up after an untidy toddler. This is all the more frustrating since the solution to the problem is so readily apparent. Why not take two attractive women and fit them with matching G-strings and leaf blowers? Then, at the end of each dance, have them blow swirling pieces of leaf-size currency into manageable little piles at the back of the stage? It's just a thought.

The next means of tip transfer was known as "the snap," and this is where things started to get a little more complicated. With the snap, a patron holds a bill out in front of him above the edge of the stage. The dancer then works her way seductively toward the patron and bends down slightly while pulling the string portion of her G-string away from her hip. The patron then eases the bill up against the dancer's hip before the dancer releases the string with a snap, thus securing the tip. I must admit, the snap allows a popular dancer to amass a little currency tutu that can be quite fetching. The problem was that most states had liquor laws that discouraged patrons from touching dancers. Meeting the letter of that law required hand steadiness more common to that of a surgeon than a half-drunk conventioneer. After a typically sloppy execution of the snap, it was not uncommon to hear a patron boast, "Didja see that? My knuckle grazed Tiffany's hip!"

I should point out that in the early 1990s most topless dancers went by the alias of Tiffany. For the minority who didn't, the more seductive Candy was the moniker of choice. Just once I would have liked to see a smokin' hot dancer strut onto the stage while the DJ boomed into his mic, "Let's hear it for Marge!"

Anyway, the final tip transfer maneuver was known as "the press," and this is where things really got dangerous. Here again, the patron holds a bill out before him above the edge of the stage. This time, however—assuming the dancer enjoyed at least average endowment—she would lean over the currency, place her hands outside each of her breasts, and then press the currency into her possession. Not only did this action strain the aforementioned liquor laws, but it gave rise to an even bigger risk. The press required that a male patron act in a completely unnatural manner. It required him to fight an urge as instinctive as a goose flying south for winter and as primal as a dog raising his leg at a fire hydrant. That urge, of course, was to grab the woman securely by the shoulders, press his face between the tatas dangling before him, and approximate the sound of a small motorboat.

Since I know this sounds extreme, I'll call your attention to the NATPE convention of 1988, still referred to in most circles as the infamous Houston NATPE. Each night of NATPE begins with an obligatory dinner. There were always enough NAPTE participants to overwhelm the good restaurants in even the biggest cities, so arrangements are made months in advance. Whether you accept an invitation to a small, informal dinner led by a single sales person, or opt into a huge group of buyers hosted by a major syndicator who has taken over an in-demand restaurant, you always RSVPed and honored your commitments. After dinner, however, you had the frat house equivalent of a free skate with tens of thousands of rowdy conventioneers unleashed on a city all at once. Some would head off to parties sponsored by the largest entertainment companies, and there were always competing venues boasting major music acts. I generally avoided these affairs, as large crowds of people made me uncomfortable, particularly when those crowds were comprised primarily of half-drunk, middle-aged, white people feigning rhythm. I was more inclined to join a small group of close friends eager to explore whatever amenities a host city had to offer. I preferred legendary old watering holes to strip clubs, but if the company was right I didn't care much either way.

One night in Houston, such a group came together. Normally I would have joined them, except that Houston was a driving rather than a walking venue. In New Orleans, for instance, you could walk the French Quarter. If things were not living up to your expectations, or if you were simply ready to call it a night, you could drift into a conversation with someone on the street and linger there while the rest of the party rambled on. Houston required that everyone pile into cars, or a stretch limo in this case, thus severely limiting such flexibility. For that reason, I opted out and joined a couple of friends who had secured a great table at one of the major hotel bars.

The next morning I was up early, pleased to feel rested and free of any hangover. After a pleasant breakfast meeting, I arrived on the convention floor just as it opened and made my way to an appointment with one of the gentlemen I waved goodbye to the night before as he headed off with the other would-be revelers. I was intercepted in front of their elaborate booth by one of our common acquaintances. He looked at me solemnly and asked, "Haven't you heard?"

"Heard what?" I replied.

Our mutual friend explained that the guys had ended up at Rick's, a cavernous topless bar on the outskirts of town. The boys were pretty wound up and made it increasingly difficult for the plain clothes cops in attendance to look the other way. Most law enforcement officials can tell the difference between real troublemakers and misbehaving business men, and no city wants to come off as inhospitable to visiting conventioneers. So Houston's finest showed great restraint, right up until one man in the party actually executed the motorboat maneuver. All seven of them, including the friend I was scheduled to meet, were in jail awaiting release. I shook my head and laughed in disbelief.

"It's not funny!" our friend protested.

"Ah, c'mon," I replied. "It's kinda funny."

As I sat that night at the Gaslight, watching Mr. High Energy flash a Jefferson in order to temp Candy into obliging him with the press, I started to wonder, could a motorboat bust be far behind?

I quickly organized a handful of bills as the next Tiffany skipped onto the stage to the beat of "Jumping Jack Flash," one of a handful of Stones hits that laid the soundtrack in most topless bars those days. Even though I had no specific training in origami, as a young art director I had tortured paper into any number of unintended uses while creating news graphics and scale models of sets. Now I furiously folded, bent, and coaxed a set of bills until I had a cylinder crowned with a smallish, torpedo-shaped cap. The cylinder was flanked by two small spheres made of carefully compressed currency. While the dancer held everyone's rapt focus, I was able to push $20 worth of a paper penis sculpture onto the stage just prior to the song's completion.

Tiffany swept up the tips offered by the patrons seated to my left before coming to my humble offering. Her mouth dropped open, she placed a free had on her chest and asked with genuine enthusiasm, "For me?" She gushed a heartfelt thank you and I responded with, "Who says chivalry is dead?"

Many stood to get a look what all the fuss was about. Some then laughed, while others starting fumbling with currency sculptures of their own. As I had hoped, my unorthodox tip created a comfortable exit point. It was much easier to leave the premises amidst high-fives and back slaps than it would have been if I had simply stated, "I'm beat and ready to call it a night." Keeping Mr. High Energy under control for the rest of the evening would be up to the gentlemen who invited him.

As I drove away from downtown, I decided that a slight buzz and utter exhaustion was probably a good thing. It might dull the senses just enough to make the Sulinda seem palatable. I then told myself to stop whining. I had stayed at some pretty lowly motels when trying to stretch my travel dollars during ski season, and the Sulinda couldn't be much worse.

Then its orange and white neon sign came into focus, as did the streetwalkers flanking its entry like dedicated sentries. Maybe they weren't actually hookers. Perhaps, along with broadcasters and home builders, a clown convention was taking place in Las Vegas and that explained the brightly-colored wigs, the faux fur coats, and the outrageous platform heels. But then again, even the most energetic clowns could not match the enthusiasm these painted ladies exhibited as they watched a thirty-something business man navigate his rental car past the Sulinda's flashing vacancy sign.

I pushed open the door to my room and was greeted by a wave of musky air that seemed equal parts stale cigarette smoke, cheap perfume, and unless I missed my guess, Arby's. As I stood there, I thought, "I'm just going to find my way into bed without turning on the lights." But I decided that whatever my imagination conjured up in the darkness was even more gruesome than the reality, so I flipped on the light switch.

I was pleasantly surprised—I had seen worse. Sure, the furniture's unique patina was courtesy of a decade's worth of glass ring marks and cigarette burns, paths were worn well into the carpet in the expected traffic patterns, and the in-wall combination heating and AC unit seemed to be held in place with duct tape, but all that was tolerable. This was particularly true if you remembered the argument made by Tom Bodette of Motel 6—their cheap rooms were indistinguishable from expensive ones once you closed your eyes to go to sleep.

It wasn't until I was preparing to actually get into bed that I was reminded of another idiom that dates back much further: the devil is in the details. Only then did I clearly see the strange pattern of stains that covered generous portions of the headboard, the comforter, the end table, and even a portion of the curtains.

I strained to recall all I'd ever known about contemporary artists like Jackson Pollock, Hermann Nitsch, and Robert Motherwell. Had any of them honed their splatter paint techniques in Las Vegas? Were any of them ever starving artists holed up at the Sulinda? Realizing the unlikelihood of my hoped for explanation, I eased back the comforter and examined the pillow case and bed sheets. Both were so grey and dingy that it was impossible to tell if they were free of the offensive stains, or if the stains simply overlapped one another to the point of making their specific outlines indistinguishable.

Knowing that January in Las Vegas could be cold and windy, I had come armed with my overcoat. I spread it across the bed, carefully positioned myself in the middle of it, and eventually dozed off to the mantra of "Stay between the stains, stay between the stains."

I awoke to a light-filled room. I remained still for a moment until I was satisfied that I had generally remained within the safe confines of my overcoat. Slowly looking around in the harsh morning light, I was surprised to find the stains were even more numerous and more clearly defined than I had realized the previous evening. In fact, as I stared upward, I was disgusted to see that the familiar splatter stains were also strewn across the ceiling—impressed, but definitely disgusted.

I tried to put all of this out of my mind as I made my way to the shower. I stood in the warm water and again employed the Tom Bodette trick, closing my eyes and pretending I was in a better place. That worked pretty well until I felt something gritty between my toes. I was relieved when I opened my eyes and found it was nothing more than loose grout getting rinsed away from the weathered tile work.

As soon as I hit the convention center floor, the indignities of the Sulinda were forgotten and after a few stress-free, afternoon appointments, I enjoyed my much anticipated reunion with my friend Donny.

In order to make the most of our time together, we agreed to head downtown. Donny had never visited that part of Las Vegas and he knew the years I logged there as a young bachelor qualified me as an adequate tour guide.

Our first stop was the Golden Gate Hotel and Casino. All of downtown Las Vegas offered an air of nostalgia, but at the Golden Gate it was so thick you could choke on it. We hit their Hofbräu first, grabbing two shrimp cocktails and two draft beers each—an indulgence that set us back a grand total of six bucks. We caught up with one another while taking in the time capsule on display before us. Mercifully, the Golden Gate was spared any attempts at modernization, making it the equivalent of a living museum. Old Vegas authenticity dripped down from ornate vintage light fixtures and oozed up through antique gaming tables. Even the employees were from what Rod Serling might have referred to as "another dimension." Dealers, male or female, wore white short-sleeved shirts with narrow black neckties. Glasses, if worn, were of the black, horn-rimmed variety. The cocktail waitresses, all veterans of the trade, were more sinewy than shapely. Cigarette smoke, first- and second-hand, contributed to their heavily-lined faces and gave the impression of cracking foundations struggling to support the complex beehive hairdos perched precariously above them.

Upon leaving the Golden Gate, we could have simply crossed Main Street to reach our next destination—the lounge at the Plaza Hotel. Instead, we first strolled down Fremont Street to take in Glitter Gulch in all its pre-walking mall glory. We admired the Golden Nugget, the Four Queens, Binion's Horseshoe club and The Mint, the four grand hotels that anchored downtown Las Vegas.

As we made our way up the opposite side of Fremont Street, the smaller venues clamored for attention, but none more conspicuously than the Gaslight. Large color posters of its dancers graced its exterior walls and a sidewalk barker even beckoned for us to come inside. Donny didn't seem to notice. I'm not sure if it was because he was completely uninterested, or if because showing interest would run contrary to his carefully cultivated personal brand. Donny was the type of guy who let a lady go first, not because he wanted to sneak a look at her rear end, but because he was a genuinely nice guy. Somehow, ogling nearly naked young women didn't fit his image. Whatever the combination of reasons, I was glad that he paid the establishment no notice.

Donny and I then crossed Main Street and made our way into the lounge at the Plaza Hotel. It was almost time for a performance by my all-time favorite lounge act, the Moon Drops.

Just as Donny considered mine to be a qualified opinion on downtown Las Vegas, he also trusted my judgment when it came to lounge acts. And why shouldn't he? I had followed them first as a Las Vegas resident, and then as a frequent visitor, for many years.

Lounge acts filled a peculiar niche in the broad spectrum of Las Vegas entertainment. On one hand, even a modest Vegas lounge act benefited from the glitz that permeated the city's entertainment scene. On the other hand, they were merely free, non-essential, atmospheric entertainment. At best, they offered welcome respite for weary gamblers. At worst, they were an unwanted distraction. In that regard, lounge acts had more in common with street performances than with the A-list acts whose names called out from the tops of taxi cabs, from across huge billboards, and from glittering hotel marquees.

A couple of the Moon Drops were on stage tuning their instruments. I explained to Donny that it was hard to know just how many Moon Drops there were. They all looked alike and moved around the stage so much that it was like trying to count energetic puppies. My best guess was that this family act featured five guys and two women, like a Pacific Islander version of the Osmonds. The guys were middle-aged with hairstyles that blended early Beatles 'dos with bowl cuts. They wore later-stage Elvis-type white jumpsuits, and while they weren't what you'd call good looking, they made up for it with confidence and swagger not seen since the days of Frank, Sammy, and Dean. The women were both pretty enough, but it was impossible to tell if they were sisters, or if perhaps, one was the mother of the crew. The most important thing about the Moon Drops was that they were actually quite good. Their vocals, while relentlessly corny, were pretty solid, and they were all capable and versatile musicians.

While we waited, I told Donny about the strangest act I had ever seen—Lola and the Man. While most lounge stages were massaged into an open space that bridged a bar with the gaming section of a casino, Lola and the Man were playing at the Four Queens, where the lounge was a small but luxurious space sequestered away from the noise of its casino. As we entered the lounge, I bet the others that comprised our party of four that the Man played an electronic keyboard allowing him to complement Lola's vocals with the cheesy synthetic sounds of the day. I was never so happy to be wrong. The Man played bass, not a cool stand-up bass, but a homely electric bass plugged into a modest amplifier. Lola wasn't so much pretty as she was what some might call handsome. That's a good thing, because the same couldn't be said for the Man. The kindest thing that could be said of their act was that it was amusing. The tunes the Man thumped out on his bass seemed to have little to do with the songs Lola's limited range allowed her to sing. It was as though they were competing, rather than collaborating. The highlight came when Lola paused between numbers to introduce a celebrity in the audience. Given that there was only one other table occupied in the lounge, she didn't need to call him out from the stage; she could have simply come down and introduced us all personally. "Ladies and gentlemen," she cried out, "let's hear it for the star of the television series, *Maude*, Mr. Bill Macy!" I suspect our overly enthusiastic ovation served only to heighten his embarrassment, but I hope not, because I've always liked his work.

As a few more of the Moon Drops fidgeted about the stage, Donny asked me if there were any rules for watching Vegas lounge acts. This was a throwback to a game we used to play when we worked together. For example, I asked Donny his rules for dealing with arrogant studio attorneys, and he asked about my rules for dealing with chief engineers with Asperger's syndrome. The answers were supposed to come in threes with a short explanation for each. I was happy to play the game again, and since the rules were not that different than the rules for visiting topless bars, I was able to recite them with ease.

"First," I said, "we don't sit too close, that way you can enjoy my running commentary of the performance." Donny smiled approvingly.

"Second," I went on, "tip the cocktail waitresses fairly and often—that way, the next watered-down drink arrives just before your last one is finished." Donny raised his glass in agreement.

"Finally," I said, "never make eye contact with a lounge singer."

Before I could elaborate, the intro to "We Are Family" erupted from the stage, signaling that the Moon Drops had arrived in all their glory. After that first installment of a typically illogical Moon Drop medley, one of the guys segued into the Beatles classic, "Got to Get You into My Life." The group generally sang without accents, but on a couple of occasions it was difficult to tell if he wanted to get us into his "life" or his "wife."

The set concluded with a surprisingly elegant and jazzy rendition of "I Get a Kick Out of You." As my focus shifted from the percussionist to the keyboard player, I became aware of the female lead singer looking in our general direction. I let my focus drift to the bass player, increasingly aware that the singer's eyes hadn't left us. I glanced over at Donny and found him lost in the moment, gazing into the eyes of the singer. He only snapped out of it when he realized she was making her way down the small stairs on the left side of the stage. Donny's expression was a mix of embarrassment and desperation. "Is she coming this way?" he asked.

With a suppressed smile I offered an almost imperceptible nod. By the time Donny looked back, she was upon him. Up close, I still couldn't tell if her age was closer to 45 or 65, but either way the heavy make-up couldn't conceal her mature beauty. And beauty was a good thing, because at the next moment, her sequined bosom pressed into Donny's shoulder as she leaned in close and cooed the lyric, "mere alcohol doesn't thrill me at all." Meanwhile her free hand arched around Donny's neck and she picked up his half-finished drink and swirled it for effect. Donny was as red as the maraschino cherry tumbling helplessly about in his glass.

"So tell me why should it be true," she continued, "that I get a kick out of you?" On the word "kick" the band thumped rather loudly and the singer slammed her sparkling hip into Donny's thigh. She made her way back to the stage just in time to finish the song, leaving Donny looking utterly stunned. Under the circumstances, I'm not sure he could appreciate that the ovation that followed was largely directed toward him.

It was a few more moments before Donny finally leaned in and asked, "So, that's why you never make eye contact with a lounge singer?"

"Yep," I replied. "That's pretty much it."

A SMASHING HOLIDAY

We would all like to think we learn from our mistakes and I certainly thought I had learned from mine. One Christmas Eve dinner, however, my family reminded me that when it came to mistakes, I was apparently a lifelong learner. We were discussing how a desert upbringing results in a greater than average number of bumps and bruises. I agreed and added, "While I was injury prone as a kid and paid a price for taking too many risks as a teenager, I'm glad my adult life has been accident free." The room fell silent. When I glanced up, everyone was looking at me as if I was as nutty as the cranberry salad I was pretending to enjoy. "What?" I asked, somewhat defensively.

Finally, my sister Janie broke the silence by politely asking, "How's that knee working out for you?"

"Oh yeah," I said, genuinely surprised at my absentmindedness. "I forgot all about the knee."

Shortly after arriving at E!, I was having a hectic Sunday night prepping to fly to Dallas for a conference. My pre-conference necessities included having a quick meeting at Johny's, a nostalgic dive diner in a then-seedy section of LA's Miracle Mile. Only upon my arrival at LAX did I realize that, after dinner, I had unwittingly left my canvas brief case, including my tickets and itinerary, lying on the running board of my restored pickup. It had to have fallen off the running board somewhere en route and, even in the unlikely event that I'd see it again, there was no time to go back and look for it now.

A quick assessment of my lousy circumstances made me realize I could buy another ticket and get my able assistant to send along a duplicate itinerary the next morning. A quick trip to most any drug or department store would at least arm me with the bare essentials and I might yet salvage the prospect of attending the busy convention.

As the concerned airline ticket agent handed me my new ticket, she said the kind of thing they used to utter occasionally before 9/11 resulted in an army of people in ill-fitting TSA uniforms at slow-moving security stations: "You'll have to run, Mr. Brannan."

And run I did. Without the burdensome weight of my beloved but bulky satchel, I built up to a respectable pace and sprinted the long, white marble titles that were the hallmark of the Delta terminal back in those days. As I reached the bottom of the long, sloping floor and started up the rise toward the boarding gates, I heard an audible "pop." My right knee didn't quite buckle on me but I stumbled into a bouncing, skipping hop until I could slow to a limping walk and stop. I looked at the astonished gate agent before me and asked, as if everything was fine, "Dallas?"

As I nursed a ginger ale on the plane, I couldn't help but notice that the swelling in my knee seemed in direct proportion to our climb in elevation. Once on the ground, I left instructions at the office for another itinerary and the overnight delivery of a few replacement essentials. The Dallas airport was so far out of town that most everything lay in between it and my hotel, including a department store that replaced a few of the niceties I was used to packing in my carry-on.

I found a doctor the next morning who armed me with a cane and said that while a tear of some sort was fairly certain, there was nothing much to do about it until I could return to LA where I would be able to rest and allow the swelling to subside.

Later that afternoon, my assistant called to say a Latino gentleman had wandered somewhat wide-eyed into E!'s trendy offices, produced one of the business cards he found in my bag, and said, in broken English, that he hoped he was returning it to the right place. Everything was there, spare cash, breath mints, calculator, and even my trusty Swiss Army knife--another of those carry-on items unthinkable today. And no, he wouldn't think of accepting a reward or even a small expression of gratitude. What a sweetheart.

Perhaps it was a good omen, because the balance of the conference went just fine, and I learned more from my business associates than I ever wanted to know about the myriad of injuries that can befall the humble knee.

Clearly, my thoroughly torn meniscus and the surgery that followed was probably not a typical example of workman's comp, but my company insisted that an executive racing on cold legs through an airport on their behalf qualified. I was never happier to live a mere one block from the office. It was the perfect physical therapy distance for transitioning from crutches, then to a cane, and finally to a limp—and it kept me from having to do the demanding, double clutch dance that operating my truck's manual transmission required.

Having conceded to Janie at the dinner table that my O.J. routine through the airport might have qualified as contributory negligence, I was prepared for a new subject when my dad earnestly asked, "How about that thing in Hawaii, was that a workman's comp claim, too?"

I sat down my utensils, turned my palms up, and examined the long, pink scars that still streaked across the fleshy base of each. "Oh, that," I said sheepishly. "Yes, the company covered those medical expenses, too."

Subsequent to the blowing of my knee, the hard-working management team at E! engaged in its annual retreat. This time it was not at the usual nice but nearby hotel resort, but given that we were hitting some major objectives, we were rewarded with having our meetings on the big island of Hawaii. The mornings involved an early attack of workshops followed by the team-building pursuits of group recreation each afternoon.

Having grown weary of watching my errant golf shots ping-pong about the otherwise beautiful volcanic boulders that lined each fairway, I opted instead one afternoon to join a few guys bound for a quiet lagoon known for its good snorkeling. I was happy with my choice. The company was good, the fish were pretty and abundant, and the water was warm.

The return left a lot to be desired, however, especially for me. The alpha male in our group noted that a swim around the point we had crossed to reach the lagoon would be a good deal shorter than the serpentine path we had walked to get there. He was right; he was also a very strong swimmer who assumed each of us was, as well.

As a native of the desert, I could butt slide in ditches with the best of them, or do nifty back-flips off the bridges that cross the canals, but slicing through an open ocean with the same beautiful strokes as the silver-backed superman at the lead was something I was ill-equipped for. This became wildly apparent when I made the mistake of cutting in too close to the shoreline and got caught in the big waves racing toward it.

Between me and the beach was a barrier of big craggy rocks. They were just like the large volcanic rocks that lined the pristine green fairways of the golf course. These, however, didn't look so beautiful to me at that moment. Like my slicing tee shots, I wished I could have bounced off those rocks, too. Instead I got raked over the first jagged rock and the sting that followed told me that a lot of scraping was happening. Probably the worst part of getting caught up between the rolling white waves of the ocean was that it gave me just enough time to ask, "How the hell did I get myself into this mess?"

It was the next big wave that really stunned me. The boiling mass picked me up and slammed me back down into an unforgiving section of rock so thoroughly that it knocked the rented swim fins right off my feet. Merely trying to keep my head above water meant I had to endure more of the same cutting and scraping until I could navigate my route to the shore.

Once I made it to the beach, I found the path that led to the resort. On the long walk back to the hotel's rental hut where we'd acquired our snorkeling gear, I noted there was nothing I could do to stop the bleeding from my shins or from the oozing pulp of my held-aloft hands.

I approached the young man in charge of the gear embarrassed and apologetic, and I immediately offered to pay for the loss of their swim fins, but he was already calling ahead to the hotel medical attendant for help. I always appreciate how medical staff, even the white-clad hotel type, are exempt from the niceties normally applied to guests under regular circumstances. I'm not sure if mine was an actual EMT or not, but he still harbored a refined sense of gallows humor. He noted that what I lacked in swimming prowess I more than made up for with my prolific shark chumming abilities.

During the next morning's meetings, I didn't raise my hand to participate in the sessions as much as usual. I knew that each time I did, my voluminous, white-wrapped hands left me looking like something comically akin to an albino lobster boy.

With that recollection, I nodded to my now smiling parents, grown siblings, and in-laws. Perhaps my predisposition for accidents had stayed with me into adulthood. It was certainly a point well made since, only hours before, my latest mishap had nearly killed me and my older brother.

With that Sunday morning's Christmas fast approaching, Doug found time on his busy Friday afternoon to fly from Phoenix in order to join me in Los Angeles so we could enjoy one of our beloved road trips together. This one would test the power steering I'd just had installed in the nicest of my series of vintage vehicles, a 1956 Ford F-100. Many consider that body style to be the apex of styling for all '50s era trucks—all I knew was that mine was fixed up just the way I wanted it. It was red, with a beautiful stock appearance on the exterior, and had just enough in the way of under-the-hood and in-the-cab updates to make it a pleasure to cruise in.

We had done a similar trip to LA from Phoenix the previous summer and were looking forward to taking the back way, well off the beaten path, on this encore trip. Knowing that we could stretch a normal six-hour freeway drive into a nine-hour extravaganza of roadside diners and junkyards, we opted for a pre-dawn, five A.M., launch time.

The bed of the truck was loaded up like Santa's sleigh with my holiday booty tied into large, black trash bags to protect it from the first light rain LA had experienced in many months.

Headlights ablaze and wipers gently swishing, we made our way east on the freeway and past downtown. We marveled at how the annual lighting of the sky scrapers, especially the tallest green one, gave the place an Emerald City quality. By the time we were safely past that distraction, we were already chatting it up while still trying to navigate the confusing confluence of the snarled exchanges that ultimately spit you eastward on Interstate 10.

Suddenly, Doug interrupted what I was saying, pointed to the illuminated overhead freeway sign, and barked "There's your turn!"

I instinctively bore right across the white line that widened in order to warn any who would try such a maneuver. There was a nice, wide off-ramp waiting, and it was a move we have all seen—and done—dozens of times, more or less safely.

Not this time. What was almost completely unique and tragically invisible through the wet darkness was a five-inch curb jutting up from the pavement between the neat, white-painted lane dividers. Our front tires slammed onto the unseen embankment and launched us over it in the general direction of the curving exit before us. The much-needed rain had been coming down just long enough to slick up the surface of the road, and even my holiday haul in the bed of the truck couldn't compensate for the front-heavy spin we slid into.

With a roadside guardrail fast approaching, I warned Doug, "I'm losin' it!" and BAMB, we slammed into the rail before spinning 360 degrees, ensuring that every corner of the truck banged the railing in rapid succession. From there, the truck somehow found its way through a rail-free section of off-ramp, allowing it to scale up an ivy-covered embankment and fly skyward. My truck then twisted in the air before it landed squarely on its roof to the shattering of glass. Then, we went into a long, grinding skid that finally came to a halt in the middle of the access road.

"You okay?" I asked, looking over at Doug, both of us hanging upside down by way of the lap belts holding us in place. He nodded that he was.

"Let's get outta here," I said completely unnecessarily given that we were both soaked in gas from the ruptured, upside down tank behind the seat. We braced ourselves with one free hand on the crushed lid of the cab beneath us and undid the airplane style latches of the lap belts biting into our waists. The effort did little to spare us the awkward tumble onto our heads and shoulders and into each other. All we needed was Curley in the middle to complete an exit through the smashed side windows in a manner the Three Stooges would have approved of.

Doug and I scrambled to the safety of the side of the road and found it relatively dry beneath the overpass up the exit road, which also allowed us to wave a warning to the first approaching driver on a mercifully light-trafficked Saturday morning.

The driver in the first approaching vehicle was in working man clothes. He dutifully hit his warning lights and pulled strategically to a conspicuous roadside warning spot for other traffic before jumping out of his truck. Looking quickly back and forth between our wet, oily, but relatively solid appearances and the battered mass of crumpled steel that lay in the middle of the road before us, he exclaimed, "You guys were in that? It's a miracle!" Then he whipped out a cell phone and called 911.

The highway patrol officer and tow truck driver who arrived on the scene shortly thereafter expressed exactly the same sentiment. Walking away unscathed from such a thoroughly battered vehicle was truly miraculous. After looking us over during the reporting procedure, the officer even deferred to me as to whether we needed an ambulance or not, but I assured him that we were just fine.

The miracle—or at least outrageous good fortune—we enjoyed was due to the early morning rain. It kept the surface of the otherwise rough, dry pavement slick enough to keep from sparking as our truck skidded along it on its hard metal roof. Without that bit of luck, we, the petrol-permeated passengers might well have been at the center of a glorious, pre-dawn, holiday fireball.

While I dealt with the officer, Doug dutifully gathered the goodies that stayed reasonably close to our wreckage and placed it all into a tidy pile for transport back in the tow truck. He even found my point-and-shoot camera among the assorted lot and did an amazing job of documenting the carnage. Perhaps most surprising was when he untied the big black bag that contained the case of home brew I still traditionally bottled up for the holidays and learned that not one of them had broken. We looked at each other in amazement and he declared, "Holy cow, now that's a miracle."

One might think that watching the sun come up as the truck was loaded onto a wrecker for transport to a salvage yard would help to bring things into a calmer, albeit more depressing mood, but the weirdness was just beginning.

The fact that the portly, ever-perspiring tow truck driver had volunteered to drop us at my apartment seemed a big bonus on what was now to be a scramble to Phoenix. That is, until his initial small talk crept further and further into the depths of bestiality and child sodomy. Seated in the middle, I scooted as firmly to my right as I could and squished Doug against the passenger door in the process. It was the kind of thing he would have rightly whacked me for as a kid, but was willing to roll with under the bizarre circumstances. Back on the street in front of my apartment, we quickly grabbed our salvaged loot and bid the driver farewell.

Once inside we shed our stinking, gas-infused adventure outfits, and I hauled them to the dumpster out back. After thorough showers, we donned what qualified as dinner attire knowing we'd be lucky just to get home without holding up the festivities. Doug called Mom to let her know what had happened and why we'd be later than expected. That's when we were both reminded of the downside of his having been the life-long, unrelenting wise guy of the family. Mom simply didn't believe him. No matter how often he stressed that he wasn't joking around, she really thought he was doing what he had done his whole life, and she refused to take the bait. Still, I think we were both surprised when he handed the phone to me, her contusion kid, and all I said was "Mom?"

I'm not sure if it was the inflection in my voice or simply a mother's intuition, but she immediately exclaimed, "Oh my gosh, you two really did have and accident, didn't you?"

A short while later we waited on Wilshire Boulevard for a bus to transport us west to Beverly Hills and the nearest car rental facility. It took a while, but one finally appeared to scoot us that way, or so I thought. As the bus driver opened the door, I lead the way through and deposited our collective fare. Before Doug could follow me in, however, the driver casually closed the door and pulled away from the curb. I looked back in shock to see Doug watching us leave him there like a lost and confused puppy. "Stop the bus!" I barked at the completely casual and nonplussed driver whose eyes never left the road. Then he pulled it back to the curb as though he knew he was leaving Doug all along.

While it's normally my nature to diffuse a situation like this, I held the driver in a menacing glare. Already that morning I had crashed my classic truck, survived a baby raping tow truck driver, and was then confronted with a bus driver who could rationalize leaving would-be riders folding their umbrellas curbside in the misty rain. As he opened the door without comment, it was all I could do not to toss his decidedly lazy ass out of it, commandeer his big blue bus, and make up for lost time en route to the Valley of the Sun. Instead, I sat down next to Doug and decided to ensure we gave our idiot driver plenty of notice for our eventual stop.

Being Christmas Eve morning, the tapped-out car rental company had but one vehicle left and it belonged to whatever level doesn't quite rise to that of subcompact. At least the tiny white Ford was the aptly named Aspire, and it lived down to its name. With a little more of everything, the anemic speck would have actually qualified as an automobile.

I navigated it back to my apartment and we crammed its modest trunk and back seat with the spoils of the morning fiasco. We headed east again, eerily passing the spot that I so hopelessly screwed up hours earlier.

Practically shoulder to shoulder in the under-powered Aspire's cramped interior, there was no reason to take the back way home. We were making up for lost time, and it was all we could do to keep up with the trucks in the slower right lane and hope that they would draft us along behind them.

Our much-anticipated classic cruise had been reduced to an emasculated and manic effort to get home in one piece in time for dinner with our family at our childhood home. And in spite of the drama of the day, it felt great to finally arrive there. That was especially true when my younger brother presented the cake he and his wife had prepared to mark the occasion. It was a sheet cake featuring an LA freeway off-ramp with a toy 1956 Ford truck placed upside down on top of it.

I should have been more upset, I guess. I killed my truck and thus depleted the ranks of a rapidly diminishing symbol of Americana in the process.

There was no denying that my family was right. I remained not just accident-prone, but rather spectacularly so even as adult. Usually a victim of my own doing, I could at least say I hadn't unwittingly killed my big brother during this process. That would have been poor form, especially on Christmas Eve.

There was another reason, however, that the holiday road trip turned out to be something special. When wrecks like ours happen, a car guy can't help but start fantasizing about his next cool ride. That is exactly how Doug and I chewed through those otherwise mundane miles, and we enjoyed it.

Maybe the Aspire was the right car after all.

A HIPPO OF
A DIFFERENT COLOR

People seem to have a love/hate relationship with Los Angeles, however, I easily came to love it. It helped that I enjoyed my work there, but I had also been so intimidated at the prospect of the infamous LA commutes that I made a point of always living within walking or bicycling distance to E!'s conveniently located midtown offices. Divorced from Lucy, I had remarried a woman named Huyen and we ended up in a lovely 1926 Spanish style home in a tree-lined neighborhood populated by a gentrifying blend of other mixed raced couples, gays, actors, and the black seniors who had saved the area when white people fled it for the suburbs decades earlier.

Simply leaving my vehicle in the embarrassingly conspicuous reserved parking spot in the network's garage was easier than having it in my way at home. If I needed to meet someone for lunch at an exclusive restaurant, my restored 1956 Willys Jeep pickup was standing by to get me there. The glistening red truck always brought a smile to the otherwise no-nonsense Latino valets who busily shuttled the ubiquitous Mercedes and BMWs in and out of the garages below. It wasn't unusual for me to exit the restaurant and find they had left my antique truck out front, showcased between a Ferrari and a Bentley whose owners probably wrongly assumed my other car was some high-end import.

In what could be an unhealthy, reality-warping environment, that old truck was an important reminder for me to remain true to the humble roots from which I had come. I guess that's why I'll always remember the day a dear friend looked at the new network president's exotic Porsche stationed next to my icon of old-school

Americana and promptly declared, "This is never going to work out."

He was right. After what was a fun, successful, and by entertainment industry standards, incredibly long run, most of the E! management team had moved on with the departure of the network's wildly popular founding president. His acting replacement was busy having her second child and charming the corporate owners while the heads of sales and legal and I kept the business churning out record ratings and revenues. When my good friend and interim president reluctantly decided to focus all her time and energy on her young family, our collective luck finally ran out.

Her replacement was a driven change agent who learned the ropes as a tough attorney at a behemoth, hard-nosed, global entertainment conglomerate. The contrasts between the beloved old president and the intimidating new one couldn't have been more striking.

Working with a new president was a challenge. E!'s business model was unique to anything she was used to. That made it necessary for me to explain and justify every detail of our programming effort over the next year, which probably sucked for both of us. After months of demanding office politics, I could not wait for my contract to end and felt its remaining six months could best be used under notice, helping her transition to a new head of programming more aligned to her way of thinking.

I waited anxiously all morning for her to return from vacation to share my decision, but to my surprise she beat me to the punch. With uncharacteristic concern, she explained her decision to bring in a mutual friend of ours to take over my duties. While feigning at least a hint of remorse seemed appropriate, getting something better than I could have ever hoped for made it easy for me to make it easy for her, and things got better again really fast.

I closed my office door, called Huyen, and said, "Sweet, I just got fired! I'm going to Disneyland!"

When big companies exercise their prerogative to replace executives without cause, it triggers an extension in their contracts to ensure they remain comfortably compensated while searching for employment equivalent to that which was just taken from them through no fault of their own. This was far superior to my expectation of simply walking away after what would have surely been an awkward, lame duck status following my planned notice.

I looked for a new position, but E! was truly a unique combination of production company and network, and little that came my way from the industry's search community was compelling to me. That was okay. I completely enjoyed relaxing at home with Huyen, pregnant with our second child, and Avery, our year-old baby boy. Festooned in swimmy diaper pants and his trademark ball cap, I'd strap him nice and tall into his car seat in my beautiful old truck and we'd cruise to the public pool at Melrose and San Vicente for swim lessons with an assortment of toddlers, their Hollywood moms, and out-of-work actor dads.

I had finally decided to worry less about the next job and develop my own show concepts to sell when I was sought out by Morley Bradford, a dapper, veteran fixture of LA's entertainment search community. He wanted to pitch me on an obscure but growing network called DgTV.

While nonplussed at first, I soon became fascinated with the potential of the little network's programming opportunities. It appealed to a small but dedicated audience of smart, technology-friendly early adopters. I could not help but think of ways to expand on their nascent efforts. The hook was set and since my time was my own, I had the luxury to obsess on just how best to move DgTV's programming agenda forward. The result was a twelve page, single-spaced strategy paper that laid out, in detail, what they needed to do and how best they could do it. Interviews were arranged at their studios in San Francisco and they seemed as excited about meeting me as I was to meet them.

Almost to my surprise, this new team was one I wanted to be a part of. While most lacked a traditional television background, they were all media experts and normal in the most refreshing sense of the word. The just-big-enough production team was shockingly good at what they did. It reminded me of how so many of the minions in LA were marking time with their day jobs while waiting for the next big thing, but that wasn't the case with the crew I encountered up in San Francisco. They liked what they did and it showed in their work. I went in expecting the location and staff to be a compromise but was thrilled to find the exact opposite was true.

The change of scenery was also great fun. The interview process included a food fest that, during which, I caught myself habitually looking over my shoulder to see who was within earshot. That had become a necessity most everywhere in the highly competitive entertainment industry town of LA. Most everything discussed over a meal was proprietary business talk, and most every restaurant featured one or two competitors. The Bay Area set, however, couldn't have cared less about television talk and it was nice to be a completely inconspicuous average Schmoe.

I'm not sure Lighting Larry O'Brien was the best boss for everyone, but he seemed perfect for me. A high-energy salesman, trim, goateed, prematurely gray, he embraced the strategy I suggested and pledged to knock the holy crap out of anything that got in our way. That sounded like a pretty good Sundance to partner up with on my latest Butch Cassidy plan of attack. There was just one rub. With the enthusiastic approval of Larry, his top teammates, and Morley, I still needed a final blessing from the network's eccentric billionaire owner, Phil Wilton.

Having enjoyed the aggressive in-house production common to local independent television, I'd always made a point of seeking out those kinds of operations after making the leap to national cable networks. What they shared in common was an unlikely mix of characters: wildly undisciplined creative types, soulless sales people, and brilliant but socially awkward engineers, all forced to toil together under one roof.

Phil Wilton definitely fell into that last category. Part of a small club of geeky young men who mainstreamed the computer industry, the bright engineer somehow ended up as one of the world's richest people. That, however, is where Phil broke away from his few contemporaries. Perhaps owing to a sense of mortality brought on by unexpected health scares, he departed a world-changing company and invested billions in his own business passions, philanthropy, and shear, unabashed self-indulgence. All in all, it proved a bit too much. While it was not yet clear to me just how differently he approached his business efforts, he was undeniably brilliant at philanthropy and self-indulgence.

His museums became calling card additions to his beloved pacific northwest and if it is true that he who dies with the most toys wins, then for anyone competing with the fantastic excesses of Phil Wilton, it was Game Over.

They booked me on a flight to meet him. I have to admit that casually knocking about with the personalities common to E!'s Hollywood focus can make you a little jaded about the celebrity set, but I was genuinely excited to meet Phil. I was eager to hear his reaction to the strategy I proposed for the network he had incorporated into his technologically-oriented vision of the future.

I arrived at the gate of his Portland compound and found it more magnificent than even those of the evil geniuses bent on world domination in the Bond movies. While he personally had a reputation as a shy introvert, most everything involving his considerable crew of handlers was designed to make an impact. I first waited in a wood-paneled lodge that conveniently housed a full-sized basketball court for visiting players from one of the professional sports franchises he happened to own. After a short time there, my khaki-clad attendant took me by golf cart along a path of equally impressive buildings before turning around in a cul-de-sac that was circled by individual glass garages, each housing rare, exotic sports cars that I had only seen in books. The building we finally stopped at was modest by comparison to those surrounding it, a charming meeting room atop a picturesque hill.

My driver showed me in, assured me someone would be along shortly, and retreated to his station outside at the cart. Someone did arrive shortly, but it was another advance man, this one setting up a notebook PC in the well-appointed technology hub that sprang up from the middle of the table. He dutifully pecked the PC into preparation and made his leave, also with a promise that someone would attend to me in short order. I waited some more until finally, the man I came to see lumbered into the room.

Admittedly, I hardly qualified as a fashion plate. I had been instrumental in establishing E!'s sister network focused on the world of style and found the level of manic insecurity among fashion designers even scarier than that of those who choose to act for a living. But by most any standard, Phil's slovenly appearance would have looked more at home in a soup kitchen than at the private island compound of Dr. No. I rationalized it as more endearing than off-putting. After all, here was a man who commissioned the building of his own private submarine and jammed on his guitar all night with the world's greatest rockers. He responded to my outstretched hand with a weak shake, almost established eye contact, and we took our seats.

Without comment, he focused on the PC screen before him, clicking its keys for a few moments before finally turning away from it and looking through the papers in front of him. The tidy stack included my strategy paper. At last, we were getting down to business.

He almost sheepishly admitted he had yet to read it. I had been so spoiled by the levels of enthusiasm and preparedness that greeted me throughout the interviewing process that I was taken aback by this bit of news. Fortunately, I was quickly able to rationalize his lack of preparedness, as well. This was one of the world's wealthiest people, and he had more important things to do than read the voluminous detail before him. Besides, I was the pro from Dover and it was time to act like it. I calmly top-lined the strategy, explained how I had done it before, and why it was going to succeed for his network. Most importantly, I made clear I couldn't wait to roll up and my sleeves and get to work.

Without really saying anything that qualified as committal, he seemed to indicate a level of agreement with what I shared, and then we exited the building to a broad sidewalk with breathtaking views of beautiful green hills and blue bodies of water. I couldn't help but note its contrast to the desert where I grew up. He mentioned doing time computer programming in New Mexico at the start of his career and recalled just wishing to see a tree once in a while. It was the most human exchange of the whole awkward interview and I was happy we shared it.

Two days later, Larry called to say Phil had given me the thumbs up and a deal was coming together. "Great!" I replied. "Did he comment on the plan?"

"Ah, well, no." Larry chuckled. "He said he thought you were a nice guy, though." If there was an odd omen in that exchange, it hadn't yet hit me.

Four weeks later and still technically a few days in advance of my contract start date, I was with the DgTV team back in Portland at Phil's corporate headquarters for our first session with him and his small, almost cultish crew of trusted insiders. With the exception of Guy Richardson, an experienced media pro willing to speak his own mind, the others in Phil's inner circle kept their eyes down and their mouths shut. Our progress report on how we were moving the agreed upon plans toward reality kept getting sidetracked by Phil's out-of-nowhere ideas, off strategy suggestions, and occasional fits of unexplainable surliness. It was as if we had never discussed anything previously, but as disconcerting as that was, I did my best to roll with it.

Back in the safe confines of our limo, I looked at Larry and asked, "What the hell was that all about?"

While others on our team looked on with genuine understanding, Larry laughed it off and said, "Oh, don't worry about it. That's how it is when you work with Phil. We call it Groundhog Day."

"Groundhog Day?" I inquired further.

"Yeah," the ever-positive Larry continued. "Phil's not exactly linear so every meeting is like starting over from a blank page. It's not particularly efficient, but you'll get used to it."

As Larry explained this, a small army of Mayflower movers was swarming over our home in LA and boxing its contents for the move to our recently purchased home in San Francisco. I blamed myself for my lack of due diligence and realized that my gift for rationalization, the one that may have just bitten me squarely on the backside, escaped me at that moment.

All things considered, Larry was right. There was no turning back for me, and the only way through was to move forward. If the plan worked, its success would render all the peculiarities of working downstream of Phil irrelevant. After all, you can't argue with success.

The exemplary team I inherited embraced my new directives with enthusiasm and no small amount of relief. They were pleased that I didn't turn out to be some LA airhead eager to blow them all out for my own cronies. Instead, I was eager to exploit their considerable talents and they appreciated finally being entrusted with their share of an easy-to-grasp bigger vision. In no time, we were having fun, it showed up in our programming, and most importantly, it was working in terms of growing ratings and increased revenues.

Unfortunately, the same couldn't be said for the drama that continued to stress the powers in Portland. It seemed the Phil-owned

202 Desert Standard Time

parent company we were part of was a major, but poorly performing, cable operator hemorrhaging billions in cash. That fact helped to explain their impatience with our modest but steady growth. The monthly meetings were increasingly uncomfortable and there was even talk of selling off the network, two full years ahead of what I suggested would be necessary to completely turn it around.

I always thought the network would be attractive to larger, more sophisticated content companies and believed it would ultimately be better off in the hands of others. But doing so at that point was like hiring a high-priced contractor to enhance the curb appeal of your shabby little abode, then putting it on the market before he could even get started.

The issue came to a boil and we again flew to Phil's gleaming glass corporate headquarters in Portland. It was a last ditch effort to avoid being sold off prematurely at a price that was hardly reflective of the potential we already showed. All the trappings of a major presentation were sent ahead of us, and as our team of five rode silently in the limo to the big showdown, the always relaxed Larry O'Brien broke the tension of what lay ahead with an absurd bet. "Look, guys, we need a little nonsense to lighten things up, a code word. The first one to drop in the word 'hippopotamus' gets fifty bucks from the others." Why not? Everyone agreed.

A harried Phil entered the meeting more disheveled than usual. His plaid shirt was only half tucked into his ill-fitting khaki pants and it sported a big blue stain on the pocket where an ink pen had recently exploded.

An oversized programming board laid out a day-parting strategy that drove our new lineup. After I reiterated its virtues, the sales and marketing heads took turns updating him on how well the lineup served their collective agendas. It didn't matter. The overriding issues with the parent company took precedent and nothing we said was going to dissuade Phil from his decision.

To emphasize his point, he reached into his pants pocket and produced an oversized, misshapen wallet, overflowing, not with cash, but with the ephemera of life. He waved it about wildly and started shouting "It's getting smaller! IT'S GETTING SMALLER!"

As absurd as the scene was, it only increased my empathy toward him. He didn't seem like one of the world's richest people at that vulnerable moment, just someone wondering how he arrived at the spot where he sat right now. It didn't matter that I desperately wanted to win, not just for me and my hard working team, but for him as well.

Only Guy Richardson of the corporate committee supported our efforts and continued funding, but he was overridden and the decision was made to put DgTV up for sale.

Since they'd made up their minds, I explained the color-coordinated, day-parted scheduling strategy posted before them was still our best option through the sales process and that we would stay the course with whatever operational funding we could retain. With a hint of defiance, I reiterated the virtues of the eclectic and intelligent mix of weekly hours in prime time, as denoted by the color orange. I explained that our second, most valuable asset was the newly edgy and irreverent content that so appealed to young men in late night. It was indicated in red. Finally, I reminded them that the technology help and informational content that was the mainstay of the network would continue to do yeoman's duty as weekday strips in daytime. While I was at it, I decided I may as well pick up an easy two hundred bucks from my friends and added that day time was highlighted in gray… *hippopotamus* gray.

It was readily apparent that I had misjudged the tension my teammates were feeling and when I surprised them with the wholly unexpected code word, they erupted into a loud and completely unexpected mass "HAAA!" They quickly regained their composure, but the damage, and the meeting for that matter, was done. The confused affair adjourned and we raced for the nearest airport bar.

Phil and company were hoping to sell DgTV to the owners of E! My former employers were planning to fold our network's bigger distribution into a fledgling video gaming network of their own.

The DgTV team was hoping for a buyer who would stay the course in San Francisco, and we made our case to a major content company that also had consumer electronics holdings of their own. Two bidders are better than one and a protracted negotiation ensued. Almost a year later, as our ratings climbed in spite of a cut in expenses, Phil garnered several times what was expected for the network. If we had simply waited and set the price point at that later moment, I believe we could have increased his return even further.

While there were opportunities to move back to LA and oversee programming efforts at networks run by both the bidding companies, I was weary of the process of disrupting my family's life. We relocated to a quiet northern California town called Woodland that was home to Huyen's family and convenient to a good airport. It remained our home and I decided to work for myself from that point on.

The sale of DgTV triggered another of those fortuitous contract clauses and I was again being paid to do nothing after being the last one in San Francisco to turn off the lights. I had enjoyed a great, but all too short time there. At least I felt vindicated by our success.

The only downside was that my code word conspirators never did come through with my well-earned two hundred dollars.

EPILOGUE

One of my first post-DgTV opportunities found me back in LA a few nights each week at a tiny apartment in Koreatown. A dashing young former investment banker had become enamored with the profit margins enjoyed by LA's big TV stations and hired me to help him create an exciting new lifestyle channel for the city.

The very definition of a bootstrapped operation, it proved as challenging as it was fun. Most importantly, it allowed me to pull together some of my favorite people from E! and DgTV while it introduced me to an ingenious new group I dubbed the Topanga Canyon Mafia.

Each morning I rode the little-known LA subway system to Hollywood Boulevard where our technical signal emanated from the glitzy corner of Hollywood and Highland, but the majority of my production time was spent a few blocks further east in a rundown, fourth floor, walk-up were our driven, young, television mercenaries worked.

While the channel failed to secure the funding it needed to keep the service in business, we managed to launch it on schedule and those who counted where impressed with the compelling mix of content we delivered with such a modest investment of cash. I was never without fun and intriguing offers of work again.

I'll always recall returning from LA to Woodland one night, leaving Sacramento's airport in my old truck of the moment, a semi-restored 1950 GMC flatbed. As was my habit, I exited the freeway for a moonlit back road home through fields reminiscent of the Mercury of my youth.

My shared office in Hollywood was in easy view of the city's legendary sign, and I was reminded that it originally had spelled out across the hilltop, HOLLYWOODLAND. The LAND portion was eventually dropped. Now I was heading to my family and our lovely old home in historic Woodland, a place that never had much HOLLY about it. All and all, life had left me pretty much in the middle of the remoteness from which I had come as well as in the excitement of where I now worked. It struck me as a lovely place to finally end up.